HUMAN RESOURCE ACCOUNTING

A COMPREHENSIVE GUIDE

DR. PRADEEP MUNDA, DR. SUNIL KR. PANDEY

To all the human resource professionals who tirelessly work behind the scenes, driving the success and well-being of every organization. Your dedication, empathy, and unwavering commitment to fostering a supportive and inclusive workplace inspire us all. May this book serve as a guiding light, empowering you to continue making a profound impact on the lives of countless individuals. This is for you—the unsung heroes of the corporate world.

Contents

Contents

Author

Dr. Pradeep Munda is a distinguished academic and educator specializing in Management and Finance. With over 16 years of teaching experience, Dr. Munda currently serves as an Assistant Professor at BIT Mesra, Lalpur Center, where he has been contributing since 2011. His extensive career includes roles as an Associate Lecturer at BIT Allahabad Campus and as a Research Associate at BIT Allahabad.

Beyond his academic responsibilities, Dr. Munda has demonstrated notable administrative prowess. He has served in several key positions including Coordinator of the Estate Management Committee, Faculty In-Charge of the Student Section, Faculty In-Charge of Security, and NSS Program Officer. His dedication to cultural and community initiatives is evident through his role as a Representative of the Hindi Cell and Coordinator of the ST cell at BIT Lalpur. Additionally, Dr. Munda has been an active member of the Eastern Zonal Cultural Center from Jharkhand, Honorary Director of the Tribal Study Center at Vikas Bharti Bishunpur, and a Governing Body member of Janyoday Vikas Parishad.

Dr. Munda's academic journey is marked by a rich blend of teaching and research. He holds an MBA and a Ph.D., with his doctoral research titled "A Critical Study of Capital Market in India with special reference to BSE." His contributions to academia and his dedication to student development are highly commendable.

Dr. Munda is a member of the Schedule Tribe and a Person with Disability, underscoring his commitment to diversity and inclusion. His distinguished career and personal dedication make him a respected figure in his field.

Awards and Recognition:

- Member, Eastern Zonal Cultural Center from Jharkhand (2014-2018)
- Hon. Director, Tribal Study Center, Vikas Bharti Bishunpur
- Governing Body member of Janyoday Vikas Parishad

Author

Dr. Sunil Kr. Pandey is an esteemed educator and researcher in the field of Management. With a profound academic and professional background, Dr. Pandey has been a dedicated member of the BIT Mesra, Patna Off-Campus, Bihar, where he currently holAds the position of Assistant Professor in the Department of Management.

Born on February 14, 1974, in Saharanpur, Uttar Pradesh, India, Dr. Pandey embarked on his academic journey with a strong foundation. He completed his Intermediate education at St. Joseph's College, Allahabad, under ISCE, New Delhi, in 1992. He then pursued a Bachelor of Arts degree from the Faculty of Arts, University of Allahabad, graduating in 1995. His quest for knowledge led him to earn an MBA from the Faculty of Management Studies, Veer Bahadur Singh, Poorvanchal University, Jaunpur, in 1999, followed by an LLB from the Faculty of Law, University of Allahabad, in 2003. Dr. Pandey's academic achievements culminated in a PhD in Management from the Faculty of Management Studies (MONIRBA), University of Allahabad, in 2008.

Dr. Pandey joined BIT Mesra on July 23, 2005, and has since been an integral part of the institution, contributing significantly to the academic and administrative landscape. His BIT Employee Code is 9800.

Dr. Pandey's contributions to academia are marked by his commitment to excellence and a deep understanding of management principles. His research and teaching have had a lasting impact on his students and colleagues, making him a respected figure in his field.

Foreword

In today's rapidly evolving business landscape, the recognition and valuation of human capital have become paramount. Organizations are increasingly acknowledging that their employees are not just a resource but a cornerstone of their success. This shift in perspective has given rise to Human Resource Accounting (HRA), a field dedicated to quantifying and reporting the economic value of human resources.

This book delves into the multifaceted aspects of HRA, providing a comprehensive understanding of its principles, practices, and significance. From enhancing decision-making and strategic planning to fostering transparency and accountability, HRA serves as a critical tool for modern organizations. By incorporating HRA into financial reporting, companies can offer stakeholders a clearer picture of their overall health and potential, ensuring compliance and building trust.

Moreover, HRA plays a vital role in employee engagement and retention, recognizing the contributions of the workforce and highlighting the importance of continuous development. Organizations that effectively manage and value their human resources can achieve a competitive edge, attracting top talent and driving long-term success.

As you embark on this journey through the world of Human Resource Accounting, you will gain valuable insights into how organizations can leverage HRA to optimize their strategies and enhance their performance. This book is an essential resource for HR professionals, financial analysts, and business leaders who seek to understand and harness the power of human capital in achieving organizational excellence.

Preface

In the ever-changing business landscape of the 21st century, organizations are beginning to realize that their most valuable asset isn't something that can be easily measured or seen. It is, quite simply, their people. Human Resource Accounting (HRA) has emerged as a groundbreaking approach that seeks to quantify the value of human capital, providing organizations with a deeper understanding of their workforce and its critical contribution to overall success.

The objective of this book is to explore the principles, methodologies, and applications of HRA in a comprehensive and accessible manner. We aim to shed light on the significance of human resources in driving organizational performance, and how HRA can be used to make informed decisions, enhance strategic planning, and foster a culture of transparency and accountability.

Throughout this book, we delve into various aspects of HRA, including its role in performance evaluation, compliance, and financial reporting. We also discuss its impact on employee engagement, retention, and talent attraction, highlighting how organizations that effectively manage and value their human resources can achieve a competitive edge in the market.

The insights and frameworks presented in this book are intended to serve as a valuable resource for HR professionals, business leaders, financial analysts, and anyone interested in understanding the economic value of human capital. By embracing the concepts and practices of HRA, organizations can unlock the full potential of their workforce, driving innovation, growth, and long-term success.

As you embark on this journey through the world of Human Resource Accounting, we invite you to rethink traditional views of accounting and finance, and to consider the profound impact that a well-valued and managed workforce can have on an organization's future.

Acknowledgements

The completion of this book on Human Resource Accounting (HRA) has been a journey filled with learning, exploration, and collaboration. I am deeply grateful to everyone who has supported and contributed to this project.

First and foremost, I would like to express my heartfelt gratitude to my family and friends for their unwavering support and encouragement. Your belief in my vision and your patience during the many hours I dedicated to this work have been invaluable.

I am profoundly thankful to my mentors and colleagues in the fields of human resource management and accounting. Your insights, guidance, and constructive feedback have significantly enriched the content of this book.

I extend my sincere appreciation to the numerous professionals, practitioners, and academics who generously shared their experiences and perspectives on HRA. Your contributions have provided a diverse range of viewpoints and have greatly enhanced the depth and breadth of this book.

A special thank you goes to my publisher, NotionPress, and the entire editorial team. Your dedication, professionalism, and meticulous attention to detail have been instrumental in bringing this book to life. I am grateful for your hard work and commitment to excellence.

I would also like to acknowledge the support of my research assistants and administrative staff. Your diligent efforts in gathering data, reviewing drafts, and managing logistics have been crucial to the successful completion of this project.

Finally, I want to thank the readers of this book. Your interest in Human Resource Accounting and your commitment to advancing the field inspire me. It is my hope that this book serves as a valuable resource in your professional journey and contributes to the ongoing development of HRA practices.

Prologue

In the early days of commerce, the success of a business was often attributed solely to the tangible assets it possessed—land, buildings, machinery, and inventory. However, as economies evolved and industries transformed, it became increasingly clear that these physical assets, though important, were not the sole determinants of an organization's prosperity. The true driving force behind innovation, growth, and sustainability lies in an often overlooked and intangible asset: human capital.

Human Resource Accounting (HRA) emerged as a response to this paradigm shift, offering a revolutionary approach to quantifying and recognizing the value of an organization's workforce. This book embarks on a journey to unravel the principles and practices of HRA, demonstrating how it provides a more holistic and accurate representation of an organization's assets and liabilities.

As we delve into the intricacies of HRA, we will explore how this field enhances decision-making, strategic planning, and financial reporting. We will examine its impact on employee engagement, retention, and talent attraction, highlighting the ways in which organizations that effectively manage and value their human resources can achieve a competitive edge in the market.

CHAPTER ONE

DEFINITION AND SCOPE

Definition of Human Resource Accounting (HRA)

Human Resource Accounting (HRA) is an approach to measuring and reporting on the value of a company's human resources. It involves quantifying the economic value of employees and their contribution to the organization's financial performance. HRA goes beyond traditional accounting by incorporating the value of employees' skills, knowledge, and abilities into financial statements, providing a more comprehensive view of an organization's assets.

Key Concepts in Human Resource Accounting

Human Capital: This refers to the collective skills, knowledge, abilities, and experiences possessed by an organization's employees. Human capital is considered an intangible asset that contributes to an organization's productivity, innovation, and competitive advantage.

Cost of Human Resources: This encompasses all expenses related to acquiring, developing, and maintaining the workforce. It includes:

- **Recruitment Costs:** Expenses incurred in attracting and hiring new employees (e.g., job advertisements, recruitment agency fees).
- **Training Costs:** Investment in employee development, such as training programs, workshops, and certifications.
- **Salaries and Benefits:** Regular compensation, including wages, salaries, bonuses, health insurance, retirement contributions, and other benefits.
- **Administrative Costs:** Expenses related to HR management, including payroll processing, HR software, and compliance-related activities.

Value of Human Resources: This represents the potential economic benefits that an organization derives from its employees' performance and productivity. It includes:

- **Employee Contributions:** The measurable output and achievements of employees that drive organizational success.
- **Future Potential:** The anticipated future benefits from employees' continued growth, learning, and contributions.
- **Impact on Financial Performance:** The influence of employees' efforts on key financial metrics, such as revenue growth, profitability, and cost savings.

Methods of Human Resource Accounting
1. Cost-Based Methods
Acquisition Cost Method:

- Focuses on the costs incurred during the recruitment and hiring process.
- Includes expenses like job postings, recruitment agency fees, interview costs, and onboarding.

Training Cost Method:

- Accounts for expenses related to employee training and development.
- Includes costs of training programs, workshops, certifications, and on-the-job training.

2. Value-Based Methods
Present Value of Future Earnings Method:

- Projects the future earnings of employees and discounts them to their present value.
- Considers factors such as performance, potential growth, and tenure within the organization.

Replacement Cost Method:

- Estimates the cost of replacing an employee with someone of similar qualifications and experience.

- Takes into account recruitment, hiring, and training expenses to bring a new employee up to the desired performance level.

Scope of Human Resource Accounting
The scope of HRA encompasses several dimensions, including:

- **Measurement and Reporting:** Quantifying the value of human resources and incorporating these values into financial statements to reflect the true worth of an organization.
- **Strategic Planning:** Using HRA data to inform decisions related to workforce planning, talent management, and investment in employee development.
- **Performance Evaluation:** Assessing the effectiveness of human resource policies and practices by measuring their impact on organizational performance.
- **Compliance and Transparency:** Ensuring adherence to regulations and standards related to human resource management and accounting, and enhancing transparency in reporting.

Benefits of Human Resource Accounting

- **Enhanced Decision-Making:** Provides valuable insights for strategic planning and resource allocation.
- **Improved Financial Reporting:** Offers a more accurate representation of an organization's assets and liabilities.
- **Increased Accountability:** Highlights the importance of human resources and encourages investment in employee development.
- **Greater Transparency:** Enhances stakeholders' understanding of the organization's human capital and its impact on performance.

Challenges in Implementing Human Resource Accounting

- **Subjectivity:** Valuing human resources involves a level of subjectivity, as it requires estimating future benefits and costs.
- **Data Availability:** Accurate data on employee performance, skills, and potential can be difficult to obtain and measure.
- **Standardization:** There is a lack of standardized methods and practices for HRA, leading to inconsistencies in reporting.

- **Cost:** Implementing HRA can be expensive and time-consuming, requiring significant investment in data collection and analysis.

Future Trends in Human Resource Accounting

- **Integration with Technology:** The use of advanced technologies such as artificial intelligence and big data analytics to improve the accuracy and efficiency of HRA.
- **Focus on Employee Well-being:** Recognizing the importance of employee well-being and its impact on productivity, leading to more comprehensive HRA practices.
- **Sustainability and Corporate Social Responsibility (CSR):** Incorporating HRA into broader sustainability and CSR initiatives to reflect the true value of an organization's human capital.
- **Globalization:** Addressing the challenges and opportunities presented by a global workforce, including cultural differences and varying regulations.

Human Resource Accounting is an evolving field that continues to gain importance as organizations recognize the critical role of human capital in driving success. By integrating HRA practices, companies can better manage their workforce, optimize performance, and achieve sustainable growth.

CHAPTER TWO

HISTORICAL BACKGROUND

Origins of Human Resource Accounting

The concept of Human Resource Accounting (HRA) can be traced back to the early 1960s, when researchers began to explore the economic value of human resources. The traditional accounting practices of the time primarily focused on tangible assets, such as machinery and buildings, while largely ignoring the value of human capital. This oversight led to the development of HRA as a means to recognize and quantify the importance of employees to an organization's success.

Early Theories and Pioneers

Rensis Likert (1960s): Likert was a key figure in the development of HRA, emphasizing the importance of human resources in organizational performance. His work highlighted the need for organizations to invest in employee development and measure the economic value of their workforce.

Eric G. Flamholtz (1970s): Flamholtz made significant contributions to the field of HRA by developing models and methods for measuring the value of human resources. His research focused on the costs and benefits associated with employee recruitment, training, and retention.

Development of HRA Models and Methods

Throughout the 1970s and 1980s, researchers and practitioners developed various models and methods to measure and report on the value of human resources. These included:

- **Historical Cost Approach:** This method involves recording the costs associated with recruiting, hiring, and training employees. It provides a straightforward way to quantify the investment made in human resources.

- **Replacement Cost Approach:** This approach estimates the cost of replacing an employee with a similar level of skills and experience. It emphasizes the economic impact of losing valuable employees.
- **Economic Value Approach:** This method focuses on the present value of future earnings generated by employees. It considers factors such as employee performance, productivity, and potential for future growth.

Integration into Financial Reporting

In the 1980s and 1990s, organizations began to recognize the importance of integrating HRA into their financial reporting. This period saw the development of guidelines and standards for measuring and reporting on human capital. Companies started to include information about their workforce in annual reports, highlighting the value of employees as a critical asset.

Challenges and Criticisms

Despite its potential benefits, HRA faced several challenges and criticisms during its early development:

- **Subjectivity:** Valuing human resources involves a degree of subjectivity, as it requires estimating future benefits and costs.
- **Lack of Standardization:** There was a lack of standardized methods and practices for HRA, leading to inconsistencies in reporting.
- **Cost and Complexity:** Implementing HRA can be expensive and time-consuming, requiring significant investment in data collection and analysis.

Recent Developments and Future Trends

In recent years, the field of HRA has continued to evolve, driven by advancements in technology and a growing recognition of the importance of human capital. Some key developments and future trends include:

- **Technology Integration:** The use of advanced technologies such as artificial intelligence and big data analytics to improve the accuracy and efficiency of HRA.
- **Focus on Employee Well-being:** Recognizing the importance of employee well-being and its impact on productivity, leading to more comprehensive HRA practices.

- **Sustainability and CSR:** Incorporating HRA into broader sustainability and corporate social responsibility initiatives to reflect the true value of an organization's human capital.
- **Globalization:** Addressing the challenges and opportunities presented by a global workforce, including cultural differences and varying regulations.

Conclusion

The historical development of Human Resource Accounting highlights the growing recognition of the value of human capital in organizational success. While there have been challenges and criticisms, the continued evolution of HRA holds promise for more accurate and comprehensive measurement and reporting of an organization's most valuable asset – its people.

CHAPTER THREE

IMPORTANCE AND BENEFITS

Importance of Human Resource Accounting

Human Resource Accounting (HRA) plays a critical role in modern organizations. The importance of HRA can be summarized in the following points:

- **Recognition of Human Capital:** Human Resource Accounting (HRA) recognizes employees as invaluable assets to an organization. It underscores the critical role they play in driving a company's success and emphasizes the necessity of investing in their growth and development. By valuing human capital, organizations can better appreciate the skills, knowledge, and expertise their employees bring to the table. This recognition fosters a culture of continuous learning and development, ensuring that employees are not only motivated but also equipped with the latest skills and knowledge to excel in their roles. Investing in human capital development leads to higher employee satisfaction, reduced turnover rates, and ultimately, greater organizational success. It's about nurturing talent, fostering innovation, and ensuring that employees feel valued and supported in their professional growth journey.

- **Enhanced Decision-Making:** Human Resource Accounting (HRA) plays a pivotal role in enhancing organizational decision-making by providing precise quantitative data on human resources. This valuable data aids in making well-informed decisions regarding recruitment, ensuring that the right talent is brought into the organization. It also facilitates effective training programs tailored to the specific needs of employees, enhancing their skills and productivity. Furthermore, HRA supports strategic workforce planning, allowing organizations to anticipate future workforce needs and make proactive adjustments. By leveraging this data-driven approach, companies can optimize their human resource management, leading to improved operational efficiency and a more agile and responsive workforce.

- **Performance Evaluation:** Human Resource Accounting (HRA) provides a structured framework for evaluating the performance and effectiveness of human resource policies and practices. This evaluation is essential for identifying the strengths and weaknesses in an organization's human resource management. By systematically assessing these policies, HRA enables organizations to pinpoint areas where improvements are needed and implement changes that enhance overall effectiveness. This optimization ensures that HR strategies are aligned with the organization's goals and objectives, leading to better employee performance, higher satisfaction, and increased productivity. Additionally, regular performance evaluation through HRA helps in maintaining transparency and accountability within the organization, fostering a culture of continuous improvement and excellence in human resource management.

- **Compliance and Transparency:** Incorporating Human Resource Accounting (HRA) into financial reporting is pivotal for ensuring regulatory compliance and enhancing transparency for stakeholders. By systematically documenting and reporting on the value of human capital, organizations can adhere to accounting standards and regulations that mandate accurate and comprehensive financial disclosures. This practice ensures that all human resource-related expenditures and investments are appropriately accounted for, providing a clear and accurate picture of the organization's financial health.

  Moreover, HRA enhances transparency by offering stakeholders, including investors, employees, and regulatory bodies, a deeper insight into the organization's workforce management and its impact on overall performance. By disclosing information about human capital investments, training programs, employee development initiatives, and workforce productivity, organizations build trust and credibility with their stakeholders. This transparency fosters a culture of accountability and openness, which can lead to more informed decision-making and stronger relationships with all stakeholders involved.

Benefits of Human Resource Accounting

The benefits of implementing HRA are manifold, including:

- **Improved Financial Reporting:** Integrating Human Resource Accounting (HRA) into financial reporting transforms how organizations portray their financial health by acknowledging the value of their human resources. Traditional financial statements typically focus on tangible assets like property, equipment, and cash reserves, while often overlooking the significant value that skilled and experienced employees contribute to the company. HRA addresses this gap by including the value of human resources as part of the organization's assets.

  By doing so, HRA offers a more holistic and accurate representation of an organization's assets and liabilities. It recognizes that the investment in recruiting, training, and developing employees should be reflected in financial statements, as these investments significantly impact the company's overall performance and sustainability. This comprehensive approach to financial reporting allows stakeholders to better understand the true value and potential of the organization, leading to more informed investment decisions and strategic planning. Moreover, it highlights the critical role of human capital in driving business success, emphasizing the need for continued investment in employee development and well-being.

- **Increased Accountability:** Human Resource Accounting (HRA) significantly enhances accountability within organizations by assigning an economic value to human resources. This quantification brings to light the critical importance of employees as key drivers of organizational success. When organizations recognize the tangible value that their workforce contributes, they are more likely to prioritize investments in employee development and retention initiatives.

  By treating human resources as valuable assets, HRA encourages companies to allocate resources towards comprehensive training programs, professional development opportunities, and employee well-being initiatives. This proactive approach not only helps in cultivating a skilled and motivated workforce but also reduces turnover rates, saving the organization costs associated with recruitment and onboarding new employees.

Furthermore, HRA fosters a culture of accountability by making it clear that investments in human capital are integral to the organization's financial health and long-term sustainability. It prompts leaders to regularly assess and improve their HR policies and practices, ensuring that they are aligned with the goal of maximizing employee potential and satisfaction. By quantifying the economic value of human resources, HRA creates a strong incentive for organizations to invest in their people, ultimately leading to enhanced performance, innovation, and competitive advantage.

- **Enhanced Strategic Planning:** Human Resource Accounting (HRA) plays a crucial role in enhancing strategic planning within organizations by providing invaluable insights into workforce trends, skills gaps, and potential areas for investment. By systematically collecting and analyzing data related to human resources, HRA helps organizations identify emerging trends in the workforce, such as changes in employee demographics, shifts in skill requirements, and evolving work preferences. These insights enable organizations to anticipate future workforce needs and adapt their strategies accordingly.

Moreover, HRA data highlights specific skills gaps within the organization, allowing leaders to design targeted training and development programs that address these deficiencies. By bridging these gaps, organizations can ensure that their employees are equipped with the necessary skills to meet current and future business challenges. This proactive approach to skill development not only enhances employee performance but also increases overall organizational agility and competitiveness.

Additionally, HRA data supports strategic investment decisions by identifying areas where additional resources are needed. For example, if the data reveals a high turnover rate in a particular department, the organization can invest in initiatives to improve employee engagement and retention in that area. Similarly, if certain roles or skills are in high demand, the organization can allocate resources to attract and retain top talent in those areas.

By leveraging HRA data for strategic planning, organizations can make informed decisions that align with their long-term goals and objectives. This data-driven approach ensures that human resource strategies are integrated into the overall business strategy, leading to improved organizational performance and sustainable growth.

- **Greater Transparency:** Human Resource Accounting (HRA) significantly contributes to greater transparency within an organization by providing stakeholders with a clear and comprehensive understanding of its human capital. This transparency is achieved through detailed reporting on various aspects of human resources, including recruitment practices, employee development programs, training initiatives, and overall workforce productivity.

  By openly sharing this information, organizations build trust with their stakeholders, such as investors, employees, customers, and regulatory bodies. Stakeholders gain confidence in the organization's management practices, knowing that it values its employees and invests in their growth and development. This trust is further reinforced when stakeholders see evidence of positive outcomes, such as increased employee satisfaction, lower turnover rates, and enhanced organizational performance.

  Moreover, greater transparency through HRA promotes accountability within the organization. When human resource data is made available, it becomes easier to monitor and evaluate the effectiveness of HR policies and practices. This visibility encourages continuous improvement and ensures that the organization remains committed to maintaining high standards in human resource management.

  Overall, HRA enhances stakeholders' understanding of the organization's human capital, fostering a culture of openness and accountability. This transparency not only strengthens stakeholder relationships but also positions the organization as a responsible and forward-thinking entity, committed to the well-being and success of its employees.

- **Employee Engagement and Retention:** Human Resource Accounting (HRA) profoundly impacts employee engagement and retention by recognizing and valuing employees' contributions. When organizations acknowledge the value of their workforce through HRA, it fosters a culture of appreciation and respect. Employees feel more motivated and committed to their work when they know that their efforts are recognized and appreciated.

  This recognition boosts morale, leading to higher levels of engagement. Engaged employees are more productive, innovative, and enthusiastic about their roles within the organization. They are more likely to go the extra mile, contributing to the overall success of the company.

Furthermore, valuing employees' contributions through HRA initiatives, such as regular performance assessments, targeted training programs, and career development opportunities, demonstrates the organization's commitment to their professional growth. This commitment to employee development not only enhances their skills and competencies but also increases their loyalty to the organization.

As a result, retention rates improve, reducing the costs associated with high turnover, such as recruitment, onboarding, and training new employees. A stable and engaged workforce is essential for maintaining continuity, preserving institutional knowledge, and fostering a positive organizational culture.

By recognizing and valuing employees' contributions through HRA, organizations create a supportive and inclusive environment that promotes long-term engagement and retention, driving sustainable growth and success.

- **Competitive Advantage:** Effectively managing and valuing human resources gives organizations a distinct competitive advantage in the market. When companies prioritize the development and well-being of their employees, they create an environment that fosters innovation, productivity, and high performance.

Investing in employee development through targeted training programs, career advancement opportunities, and continuous learning initiatives ensures that the workforce is equipped with the latest skills and knowledge. This not only enhances individual performance but also drives collective organizational success. A well-trained and motivated workforce can adapt quickly to market changes, implement new technologies, and innovate solutions that give the organization an edge over competitors.

Moreover, organizations that value their human resources tend to have higher employee satisfaction and retention rates. A stable and engaged workforce reduces the costs and disruptions associated with high turnover, ensuring continuity and preserving institutional knowledge. Satisfied employees are more likely to be loyal brand ambassadors, positively influencing the organization's reputation in the market.

Additionally, a strong focus on human resource management builds a positive organizational culture that attracts top talent. Companies known for their commitment to employee well-being and development are often seen as desirable employers, making it easier to recruit and retain high-caliber professionals. This talent pool further contributes to the organization's competitive strength.

In summary, organizations that effectively manage and value their human resources create a sustainable competitive advantage by fostering innovation, enhancing productivity, maintaining stability, and attracting top talent. These factors collectively drive long-term success and market leadership.

- **Attraction of Talent:** Transparent reporting of human resource value through Human Resource Accounting (HRA) plays a significant role in attracting top talent to an organization. Potential employees, especially those with high levels of skill and experience, are increasingly looking for workplaces that genuinely value and invest in their workforce. By providing clear and honest information about how the organization values and manages its human resources, companies can demonstrate their commitment to employee development, well-being, and growth.

  When potential employees see that an organization transparently reports on aspects such as training programs, career development opportunities, employee satisfaction, and retention rates, they are more likely to be attracted to the organization. This transparency signals that the company prioritizes its workforce and is dedicated to creating a positive and supportive work environment.

  Moreover, transparent reporting helps to build the organization's reputation as an employer of choice. Talented professionals are more likely to seek out companies that are known for their ethical practices, commitment to employee growth, and fair treatment of their workforce. By highlighting the value placed on human resources, organizations can differentiate themselves from competitors and attract top-tier candidates who are looking for a long-term and fulfilling career.

  In essence, HRA's transparent reporting of human resource value serves as a powerful tool for talent attraction, helping organizations build a strong, skilled, and motivated workforce that drives their success and innovation.

Case Studies and Examples

Infosys Limited: Infosys, an Indian multinational corporation, has been a pioneer in incorporating HRA into its annual reports. The company quantifies its human resources based on the present value of future earnings, providing stakeholders with valuable insights into its workforce's economic contribution.

Tata Consultancy Services (TCS): TCS, another Indian multinational corporation, emphasizes the importance of human capital in its financial reporting. By integrating HRA practices, TCS showcases its commitment to employee development and well-being.

Challenges in Implementing HRA

Despite its benefits, implementing HRA can be challenging due to the following factors:

- **Data Collection:** Accurate and comprehensive data on employee performance, skills, and potential can be difficult to obtain.
- **Subjectivity:** Valuing human resources involves subjective estimates of future benefits and costs.
- **Standardization:** The lack of standardized methods and practices for HRA can lead to inconsistencies in reporting.
- **Cost and Complexity:** Implementing HRA requires significant investment in data collection, analysis, and reporting.

Addressing Challenges in HRA

To overcome these challenges, organizations can adopt the following strategies:

- **Use of Technology:** Leveraging advanced technologies, such as artificial intelligence and big data analytics, can improve the accuracy and efficiency of HRA.
- **Standardization of Methods:** Developing and adopting standardized methods and practices for HRA can enhance consistency in reporting and comparability across organizations.
- **Training and Development:** Investing in training and development programs for HR professionals can improve their ability to collect and analyze HRA data effectively.
- **Collaboration with Experts:** Engaging with HRA experts and researchers can provide valuable insights and guidance on best practices and emerging trends.

Future Trends in Human Resource Accounting

The field of HRA is continuously evolving, with several future trends shaping its development:

- **Integration with HR Technology:** The adoption of HR technology platforms that incorporate HRA data to provide real-time insights into workforce performance and potential.
- **Focus on Employee Well-being:** Recognizing the importance of employee well-being and mental health, and incorporating these factors into HRA practices.
- **Sustainability and CSR Initiatives:** Integrating HRA into broader sustainability and corporate social responsibility initiatives to reflect the true value of an organization's human capital.
- **Global Workforce Management:** Addressing the challenges and opportunities presented by a global workforce, including managing diverse talent pools and complying with varying regulations.

Conclusion

Human Resource Accounting is essential for recognizing and valuing an organization's most significant asset—its people. By providing a comprehensive view of human capital, HRA enhances decision-making, transparency, and strategic planning. Despite challenges, the benefits of HRA make it a valuable tool for modern organizations committed to optimizing their workforce and achieving sustainable growth.

Importance of Human Resource Accounting

Human Resource Accounting (HRA) plays a critical role in modern organizations. The importance of HRA can be summarized in the following points:

- **Recognition of Human Capital:** HRA highlights the value of employees as significant assets, emphasizing the importance of investing in their development.
- **Enhanced Decision-Making:** By providing quantitative data on human resources, HRA aids in informed decision-making related to recruitment, training, and workforce planning.
- **Performance Evaluation:** HRA offers a framework for assessing the effectiveness of human resource policies and practices, enabling organizations to optimize their strategies.

- **Compliance and Transparency:** Incorporating HRA into financial reporting ensures adherence to regulations and enhances transparency for stakeholders.

Benefits of Human Resource Accounting

The benefits of implementing HRA are manifold, including:

- **Improved Financial Reporting:** HRA provides a more accurate representation of an organization's assets and liabilities by including the value of human resources in financial statements.
- **Increased Accountability:** By quantifying the economic value of human resources, HRA encourages organizations to invest in employee development and retention.
- **Enhanced Strategic Planning:** HRA data supports strategic planning by offering insights into workforce trends, skills gaps, and potential areas for investment.
- **Greater Transparency:** HRA enhances stakeholders' understanding of the organization's human capital, fostering trust and confidence.
- **Employee Engagement and Retention:** Recognizing and valuing employees' contributions can boost morale, engagement, and retention.
- **Competitive Advantage:** Organizations that effectively manage and value their human resources can achieve a competitive edge in the market.
- **Attraction of Talent:** Transparent reporting of human resource value can attract top talent, as potential employees seek organizations that prioritize their workforce.

Case Studies and Examples

Infosys Limited: Infosys, an Indian multinational corporation, has been a pioneer in incorporating HRA into its annual reports. The company quantifies its human resources based on the present value of future earnings, providing stakeholders with valuable insights into its workforce's economic contribution.

Tata Consultancy Services (TCS): TCS, another Indian multinational corporation, emphasizes the importance of human capital in its financial reporting. By integrating HRA practices, TCS showcases its commitment to employee development and well-being.

Challenges in Implementing HRA

Despite its benefits, implementing HRA can be challenging due to the following factors:

- **Data Collection:** Accurate and comprehensive data on employee performance, skills, and potential can be difficult to obtain.
- **Subjectivity:** Valuing human resources involves subjective estimates of future benefits and costs.
- **Standardization:** The lack of standardized methods and practices for HRA can lead to inconsistencies in reporting.
- **Cost and Complexity:** Implementing HRA requires significant investment in data collection, analysis, and reporting.

Addressing Challenges in HRA

To overcome these challenges, organizations can adopt the following strategies:

- **Use of Technology:** Leveraging advanced technologies, such as artificial intelligence and big data analytics, can improve the accuracy and efficiency of HRA.
- **Standardization of Methods:** Developing and adopting standardized methods and practices for HRA can enhance consistency in reporting and comparability across organizations.
- **Training and Development:** Investing in training and development programs for HR professionals can improve their ability to collect and analyze HRA data effectively.
- **Collaboration with Experts:** Engaging with HRA experts and researchers can provide valuable insights and guidance on best practices and emerging trends.

Future Trends in Human Resource Accounting

The field of HRA is continuously evolving, with several future trends shaping its development:

- **Integration with HR Technology:** The adoption of HR technology platforms that incorporate HRA data to provide real-time insights into workforce performance and potential.
- **Focus on Employee Well-being:** Recognizing the importance of employee well-being and mental health, and incorporating these factors

into HRA practices.

- **Sustainability and CSR Initiatives:** Integrating HRA into broader sustainability and corporate social responsibility initiatives to reflect the true value of an organization's human capital.
- **Global Workforce Management:** Addressing the challenges and opportunities presented by a global workforce, including managing diverse talent pools and complying with varying regulations.

Conclusion

Human Resource Accounting is essential for recognizing and valuing an organization's most significant asset—its people. By providing a comprehensive view of human capital, HRA enhances decision-making, transparency, and strategic planning. Despite challenges, the benefits of HRA make it a valuable tool for modern organizations committed to optimizing their workforce and achieving sustainable growth.

CHAPTER FOUR

CONCEPTS AND THEORIES

Key Concepts in Human Resource Accounting

Human Resource Accounting (HRA) encompasses various concepts that provide a foundation for measuring and reporting the value of human resources. Some of the key concepts include:

- **Human Capital:** Human capital represents the collective skills, knowledge, abilities, and experiences of an organization's workforce. It underscores the notion that employees are not merely expendable resources but valuable assets that drive innovation, productivity, and overall organizational success. By investing in human capital through training, development, and engagement initiatives, organizations can enhance their competitive edge, foster growth, and achieve sustainable success. In essence, human capital is a critical factor in maximizing an organization's potential and achieving its strategic objectives.

- **Cost of Human Resources:** This concept involves quantifying the total expenses incurred by an organization in recruiting, hiring, training, and maintaining employees. It encompasses a wide range of costs, including advertising for job vacancies, recruitment agency fees, interview expenses, background checks, onboarding programs, and ongoing training and development initiatives. Additionally, it includes regular compensation such as salaries, wages, bonuses, health insurance, retirement benefits, and other employee perks. Administrative costs related to managing HR functions, such as payroll processing, HR software, and compliance activities, are also part of this calculation. Understanding these costs helps organizations evaluate the efficiency of their HR practices, justify investments in employee development, optimize budget planning, and make informed, data-driven decisions to enhance workforce performance and retention.

- **Value of Human Resources:** This concept centers on the potential economic benefits generated by employees through their performance, skills, and productivity. It emphasizes the importance of recognizing and measuring the contributions that human resources make to the organization's success. By evaluating the value of human resources, organizations can gain insights into how employees drive revenue growth, innovation, and competitive advantage. This involves not only assessing current performance but also forecasting future potential and contributions. Understanding the value of human resources helps organizations make informed decisions about investments in training, development, and employee engagement initiatives. Ultimately, it underscores the critical role that employees play in achieving strategic goals and sustaining long-term growth.

Theories in Human Resource Accounting

Several theories have been developed to explain and support the practice of Human Resource Accounting. These theories provide a framework for understanding the importance of human resources and their impact on organizational performance. Some of the prominent theories include:

- **Human Capital Theory:** Developed by economists Gary Becker and Theodore Schultz, the Human Capital Theory posits that investments in education, training, and development significantly enhance an individual's skills, knowledge, and abilities. These investments lead to increased productivity, higher earnings, and greater economic value. The theory emphasizes that just as physical capital (like machinery) requires investment to yield returns, so too does human capital. By investing in employees' education and skill development, organizations can boost their overall performance, foster innovation, and maintain a competitive edge in the market. This theory underscores the critical role of continuous learning and development in driving organizational success and economic growth.

- **Resource-Based View (RBV) Theory:** The Resource-Based View (RBV) theory, proposed by Jay Barney, posits that an organization's resources, including human resources, are fundamental to gaining and sustaining a competitive advantage. According to this theory, human resources must possess four key attributes to contribute to a competitive edge: they must be valuable, enabling the organization to improve efficiency and effectiveness; rare, meaning they are not easily obtainable by competitors; inimitable, indicating that they are difficult for competitors to replicate due to unique qualities; and non-substitutable, meaning there are no readily available alternatives that can provide the same benefits. By focusing on these characteristics, the RBV theory underscores the importance of human resources as unique assets that drive long-term organizational success and differentiation in the marketplace.

- **Social Exchange Theory:** Developed by George Homans, Social Exchange Theory posits that relationships between individuals and organizations are based on reciprocal exchanges and mutual benefits. In the context of Human Resource Accounting (HRA), this theory suggests that when organizations invest in their employees' well-being, development, and overall work experience, they are likely to receive higher levels of commitment, loyalty, and performance in return. The theory highlights the importance of a give-and-take relationship, where employees feel valued and supported by their organization, leading to increased motivation and engagement. In essence, Social Exchange Theory underscores the idea that positive investments in employees create a cycle of reciprocation, fostering a more productive and harmonious work environment.

- **Contingency Theory:** Proposed by Joan Woodward, Contingency Theory posits that the effectiveness of human resource practices is contingent upon the specific context and environment in which an organization operates. This theory argues that there is no one-size-fits-all approach to human resource management; instead, HR practices must be tailored to align with the unique circumstances, cultural dynamics, and strategic objectives of each organization. For instance, what works well for a tech startup in Silicon Valley may not be effective for a manufacturing firm in the Midwest. By adapting HRA practices to fit the organizational context, companies can enhance their effectiveness, responsiveness, and overall performance. This theory underscores the importance of flexibility and customization in designing HR strategies that cater to an organization's distinct needs and goals.

Application of Concepts and Theories in HRA

- **Human Capital Measurement:** Organizations employ a variety of methods to quantify the value of their human capital. These methods often involve assessing employee skills, knowledge, competencies, and overall performance. For example, performance appraisals, 360-degree feedback, and skills inventories are commonly used to evaluate employee capabilities and contributions. Additionally, organizations may utilize quantitative metrics, such as productivity ratios and output per employee, to gauge the economic impact of their workforce. By measuring human capital, organizations can identify strengths and areas for improvement, allocate resources effectively, and make informed decisions about investments in training and development. This helps in maximizing employee potential, enhancing organizational performance, and achieving strategic goals.

- **Cost Analysis:** By thoroughly examining the costs associated with human resources, organizations can pinpoint inefficiencies and identify opportunities to optimize investments. This process involves analyzing various expenses such as recruitment, training, salaries, benefits, and administrative costs. Through cost analysis, organizations can uncover patterns and trends, enabling them to make data-driven decisions that enhance operational efficiency and allocate resources more effectively. Additionally, cost analysis plays a crucial role in budgeting and financial planning by providing a clear understanding of the financial implications of HR activities. It helps organizations forecast future expenses, set realistic budgets, and ensure that HR investments align with strategic objectives, ultimately contributing to overall organizational performance and sustainability.

- **Value Assessment:** This process involves evaluating the potential economic benefits that human resources bring to an organization. By projecting future earnings, productivity, and contributions, organizations can quantify the financial impact of their workforce. Value assessment encompasses various methods, such as forecasting future revenue generated by employees, estimating the economic value of their skills and knowledge, and analyzing their role in achieving strategic objectives. This assessment is crucial for strategic planning, as it helps organizations identify high-potential employees, allocate resources effectively, and set performance benchmarks. Additionally, value assessment supports performance evaluation by providing a data-driven basis for recognizing and rewarding employee contributions, ultimately fostering a culture of growth and excellence.

- **Strategic Planning:** The concepts and theories of Human Resource Accounting (HRA) are instrumental in informing strategic planning by offering valuable insights into workforce trends, identifying skills gaps, and pinpointing potential areas for investment. By leveraging HRA data, organizations can develop targeted strategies for recruitment, ensuring they attract talent with the right skills and competencies to meet future demands. Additionally, HRA helps in designing effective training programs that address existing skill deficiencies and prepare employees for emerging challenges. Retention strategies are also strengthened through HRA, as it provides a clear understanding of factors that contribute to employee satisfaction and engagement. Overall, the integration of HRA into strategic planning enables organizations to make informed decisions that align with their long-term goals, optimize resource allocation, and drive sustained growth and performance.

Challenges in Applying Concepts and Theories

- **Data Availability:** Obtaining accurate and comprehensive data on employee performance, skills, and potential can be challenging for organizations. Factors such as inconsistent data collection methods, lack of standardized metrics, and privacy concerns can hinder the availability of reliable data. Additionally, subjective assessments and biases in performance evaluations can impact the accuracy of the data. Ensuring the availability of high-quality data requires implementing robust HR information systems, adopting standardized evaluation frameworks, and fostering a culture of transparency and continuous feedback. Access to accurate data is essential for effective Human Resource Accounting, as it enables organizations to make informed decisions, identify skill gaps, and invest in employee development to drive overall organizational performance.

- **Subjectivity:** Valuing human resources often involves subjective estimates and judgments, which can lead to inconsistencies in measurement and reporting. Factors such as performance appraisals, potential assessments, and skill evaluations are inherently subjective and can vary based on the evaluator's perspective and biases. This subjectivity can impact the accuracy and reliability of Human Resource Accounting data, making it challenging to standardize valuations across different contexts. To mitigate these issues, organizations can adopt standardized evaluation frameworks, ensure transparency in assessment processes, and provide training to minimize biases. Accurate and consistent valuation of human resources is essential for effective decision-making and strategic planning.

- **Standardization:** The absence of standardized methods and practices in Human Resource Accounting (HRA) can lead to significant variations in how organizations measure and report human capital. Without a uniform framework, different organizations may adopt disparate approaches to valuing their workforce, making it difficult to compare data and benchmark performance across industries. These variations can result in inconsistencies in financial reporting, decision-making, and strategic planning. To address this challenge, there is a growing need for the development of standardized guidelines and best practices for HRA. Standardization can enhance transparency, improve the reliability of data, and facilitate more accurate comparisons, ultimately supporting better-informed decisions and fostering a more cohesive understanding of human capital's value.

- **Cost and Complexity:** Implementing Human Resource Accounting (HRA) practices necessitates a considerable investment in data collection, analysis, and reporting. The process involves gathering detailed and accurate information on employee performance, skills, and potential, which can be time-consuming and resource-intensive. Additionally, the complexity of analyzing this data to produce meaningful insights requires advanced analytical tools and expertise. Smaller organizations or those with limited resources may find it challenging to allocate the necessary funds and personnel to effectively implement HRA practices. Despite these challenges, the benefits of accurate HRA—such as improved strategic planning, better resource allocation, and enhanced workforce management—can provide significant returns on investment for organizations that commit to this approach.

Conclusion

The concepts and theories of Human Resource Accounting provide a robust framework for understanding and measuring the value of human resources. By applying these concepts and theories, organizations can enhance their decision-making, strategic planning, and performance evaluation. Despite challenges, the continued development and application of HRA practices hold promise for more accurate and comprehensive measurement and reporting of an organization's most valuable asset—its people.

CHAPTER FIVE

HUMAN CAPITAL THEORY

Introduction to Human Capital Theory

Human Capital Theory is a fundamental framework that emphasizes the importance of investing in human resources to enhance individual and organizational performance. Developed by economists such as Gary Becker and Theodore Schultz, this theory posits that human capital—comprising skills, knowledge, and abilities—plays a critical role in driving economic growth and productivity.

Key Principles of Human Capital Theory

- **Investment in Education and Training:** Human Capital Theory, developed by economists such as Gary Becker and Theodore Schultz, emphasizes that investments in education, training, and development significantly enhance an individual's skills and abilities. These investments lead to increased productivity, higher earnings, and greater economic value for both individuals and organizations. When organizations allocate resources to employee development, such as funding for advanced education, certification programs, and continuous training, they effectively build a more competent and capable workforce. This, in turn, drives higher levels of performance, innovation, and efficiency within the organization. Investing in employee development not only yields immediate benefits in terms of improved job performance but also contributes to long-term growth by fostering a culture of learning and adaptability. Organizations that prioritize such investments can expect better retention rates, enhanced employee satisfaction, and ultimately, higher returns on their investment in human capital.

- **Economic Value of Human Capital:** Human Capital Theory underscores that human capital is a valuable asset with measurable economic worth. By quantifying the economic benefits derived from employees' skills, knowledge, and abilities, organizations can gain a clearer understanding of the financial impact of their workforce. This involves evaluating how employees' contributions translate into revenue growth, cost savings, and enhanced productivity. By doing so, organizations can make informed decisions about where to allocate resources, such as investing in training and development programs, to maximize returns. Moreover, this assessment supports strategic planning by identifying critical skill gaps and future talent needs, helping organizations stay competitive and achieve long-term success. Ultimately, recognizing the economic value of human capital enables organizations to optimize their human resource investments and drive overall performance.

- **Continuous Learning and Development:** Human Capital Theory underscores the critical role of continuous learning and development in maintaining and enhancing an individual's skills, knowledge, and abilities. By fostering a culture of continuous improvement, organizations can ensure that their workforce remains adaptable, innovative, and capable of meeting emerging challenges. This involves providing opportunities for ongoing education, training, skill-building, and professional growth. Organizations that invest in continuous learning not only enhance their employees' competencies but also drive higher levels of engagement, job satisfaction, and retention. Such investments contribute to sustainable growth and competitiveness, as employees are better equipped to innovate, improve processes, and contribute to the organization's strategic goals. In essence, a commitment to continuous learning and development enables organizations to build a dynamic and resilient workforce that can thrive in an ever-evolving business landscape.

- **Return on Investment (ROI):** Human Capital Theory posits that investments in human capital, such as education, training, and employee development, yield significant returns in the form of increased productivity, innovation, and profitability. By enhancing employees' skills and knowledge, organizations can achieve higher levels of performance and operational efficiency. Measuring the ROI of these investments involves assessing the tangible and intangible benefits gained relative to the costs incurred. This includes evaluating improvements in employee performance, reduction in turnover rates, increased revenue, and enhanced competitive advantage. By quantifying the ROI of human capital investments, organizations can determine the effectiveness of their development programs, justify resource allocation, and make informed decisions to optimize their workforce strategies for sustainable growth and success.

Application of Human Capital Theory in Organizations

- **Workforce Planning:** Human Capital Theory plays a pivotal role in workforce planning by identifying skills gaps and areas that require investment in employee development. By analyzing the current capabilities of the workforce and comparing them with future needs, organizations can pinpoint specific competencies that are lacking and plan accordingly. This information helps in designing targeted recruitment strategies to attract talent with the necessary skills. Additionally, it informs the development of tailored training programs to enhance existing employees' competencies and prepare them for future challenges. Effective workforce planning also involves retention strategies to ensure that valuable employees remain with the organization. By leveraging insights from Human Capital Theory, organizations can create a dynamic and responsive workforce that aligns with their long-term strategic objectives and adapts to evolving market demands.

- **Performance Management:** Human Capital Theory offers a valuable framework for evaluating employee performance and potential, enabling organizations to make data-driven decisions about key HR practices. By assessing the economic value that employees bring through their skills, knowledge, and contributions, organizations can determine the most effective ways to promote, reward, and develop their workforce. This involves using metrics and performance evaluations to measure individual and team achievements, identify high-performing employees, and recognize areas for improvement. With these insights, organizations can implement targeted career development programs, design fair and motivating reward systems, and make informed decisions about promotions. Ultimately, this approach ensures that investments in human capital yield maximum returns by fostering a culture of excellence and continuous improvement.

- **Talent Management:** Human Capital Theory underscores the significance of attracting, retaining, and developing top talent as a critical factor in achieving a competitive advantage. Organizations that excel in talent management create strategies to identify and recruit high-potential candidates, provide continuous opportunities for skill enhancement, and foster an environment that nurtures employee growth and satisfaction. By prioritizing talent management, companies can build a strong and adaptable workforce capable of driving innovation, efficiency, and success. Effective talent management not only enhances individual performance but also contributes to the organization's long-term goals, ensuring sustainable growth and a solid market position.

- **Strategic Human Resource Management (HRM):** Human Capital Theory plays a crucial role in supporting strategic HRM by ensuring that investments in human capital are closely aligned with organizational goals. By integrating this theory into HRM practices, organizations can develop a comprehensive approach to managing their workforce that focuses on maximizing the value and potential of their employees. This involves aligning recruitment, training, development, and retention strategies with the organization's long-term objectives, thereby creating a cohesive and motivated workforce that drives overall success. Strategic HRM emphasizes the importance of continuously assessing and enhancing employee skills, fostering a culture of innovation and adaptability, and ensuring that HR practices are responsive to the evolving needs of the business. By adopting this approach, organizations can optimize their human capital, improve performance, and achieve sustainable competitive advantage in the market.

Case Studies and Examples

- **Google:** is highly regarded for its commitment to employee development and continuous learning, which forms a cornerstone of its corporate culture. The company provides an array of training programs that span technical skills, leadership development, and personal growth. Employees have access to numerous resources, including online courses, in-house workshops, and external certifications, to continuously enhance their capabilities.

Mentorship opportunities are another key aspect of Google's approach, with employees encouraged to seek guidance from experienced colleagues to foster their professional growth. Additionally, Google offers comprehensive career development resources, such as career coaching, performance feedback, and individualized development plans, ensuring that employees have the support they need to advance their careers within the organization.

This strong emphasis on human capital investment not only attracts top talent but also cultivates a high level of innovation and productivity. Google's dedication to its employees' growth and well-being has earned it a reputation as one of the best places to work, consistently ranking high in employer surveys and achieving impressive business outcomes.

- **Infosys Limited:** Infosys Limited, a prominent Indian multinational corporation, exemplifies the application of Human Capital Theory through substantial investments in its employees' education and training. At the heart of this initiative is the Infosys Global Education Center in Mysore, India, which is renowned for its comprehensive training programs. New hires undergo rigorous induction and training to equip them with the skills needed to excel in their roles. Additionally, the center offers continuous learning opportunities for existing employees, ensuring they remain updated with the latest industry trends and technological advancements. This steadfast commitment to employee development not only enhances individual competencies but also drives the overall success and growth of Infosys in the competitive IT industry. By prioritizing human capital, Infosys has built a skilled and adaptable workforce that contributes significantly to its innovative solutions and global market leadership.

Challenges in Implementing Human Capital Theory

- **Measurement and Evaluation:** Accurately measuring the economic value of human capital and assessing the return on investment (ROI) of investments in education and training can indeed be challenging. This complexity arises due to the intangible and multifaceted nature of human capital. Factors such as employee skills, knowledge, experience, and productivity are not easily quantifiable. Additionally, the benefits of investments in education and training often manifest over the long term, making it difficult to directly correlate these investments with immediate financial outcomes. Organizations need to employ a combination of qualitative and quantitative methods to evaluate the impact of human capital investments. This may include performance metrics, employee feedback, productivity ratios, and advanced analytical tools. Despite the challenges, accurate measurement and evaluation are crucial for making informed decisions about resource allocation, enhancing workforce development strategies, and ultimately driving organizational success.

- **Resource Constraints:** Limited financial and organizational resources can significantly hinder an organization's ability to invest in comprehensive employee development programs. Budgetary restrictions may prevent companies from offering extensive training opportunities, advanced educational courses, or continuous learning initiatives. Additionally, constraints on human resources—such as a lack of dedicated training personnel or insufficient time for employees to participate in development activities—can further impede the implementation of robust training programs. These limitations may lead to skill gaps, reduced employee engagement, and diminished overall performance. Organizations facing resource constraints must prioritize their investments strategically, focusing on high-impact areas and leveraging cost-effective methods like online learning platforms, in-house training sessions, and mentorship programs to maximize the development of their workforce within available resources.

- **Changing Skill Requirements:** In today's fast-paced world, rapid technological advancements and shifting market demands continuously reshape the skill requirements for employees. As new technologies emerge and industries evolve, organizations must ensure that their workforce remains equipped with the relevant knowledge and competencies. This necessitates a proactive approach to training and development, with regular updates to programs that address these changing needs. Employees must be given opportunities for continuous learning to stay current with the latest tools, techniques, and industry best practices. By investing in ongoing education and skill enhancement, organizations can maintain a competitive edge, drive innovation, and ensure that their workforce is adaptable and prepared for future challenges. This approach not only benefits the organization but also empowers employees to grow and succeed in their careers.

Future Trends in Human Capital Theory

- **Technology Integration:** The integration of advanced technologies like artificial intelligence (AI) and big data analytics has revolutionized the way organizations measure and develop human capital. AI-powered tools can analyze vast amounts of employee data, identifying patterns and trends that might not be visible through traditional methods. These insights help in making more accurate and informed decisions about recruitment, training, and performance management. Big data analytics enables organizations to process and interpret large datasets, providing a comprehensive view of workforce capabilities and potential. By leveraging these technologies, companies can enhance the accuracy and efficiency of human capital measurement, tailor development programs to individual needs, and predict future skill requirements. This approach not only optimizes the use of human resources but also fosters a culture of continuous improvement and innovation.

- **Focus on Soft Skills:** Recognizing the importance of soft skills alongside technical skills is crucial for holistic employee development and organizational success. Soft skills, such as communication, leadership, teamwork, problem-solving, and emotional intelligence, play a vital role in fostering a positive work environment, enhancing collaboration, and driving innovation. Employees with strong soft skills are better equipped to navigate complex interpersonal dynamics, lead teams effectively, and adapt to changing circumstances. Investing in the development of these skills through training programs, workshops, and coaching can lead to higher employee engagement, improved customer satisfaction, and greater overall productivity. Organizations that prioritize both technical and soft skills development create a well-rounded, versatile workforce capable of achieving long-term success and maintaining a competitive edge in the market.

- **Employee Well-being:** Prioritizing employee well-being and mental health is essential for enhancing productivity and overall performance within an organization. A positive work environment that supports physical, emotional, and mental health can lead to higher levels of job satisfaction, reduced absenteeism, and increased employee engagement. Strategies to promote well-being include offering flexible work arrangements, providing access to mental health resources and counseling, encouraging work-life balance, and creating a supportive and inclusive workplace culture. When employees feel valued and cared for, they are more likely to be motivated, focused, and productive. Investing in employee well-being not only benefits individuals but also contributes to the organization's long-term success by fostering a healthier, happier, and more resilient workforce.

- **Global Workforce Management:** Managing a global workforce comes with unique challenges and opportunities, including cultural differences and varying regulations. Cultural diversity brings a wealth of perspectives that can drive innovation but can also lead to misunderstandings without proper awareness and sensitivity training. Varying labor laws, tax regulations, and employment standards across countries require organizations to navigate complex compliance landscapes, often demanding specialized expertise. Effective communication is crucial, leveraging technology to bridge time zones and geographical barriers while ensuring clear, consistent messaging. Talent management strategies must be tailored to local market conditions and cultural nuances, with a focus on competitive compensation, career development, and work-life balance. The rise of remote work further complicates engagement and productivity, necessitating robust remote policies and strong virtual culture. Managing employee mobility for international assignments and business travel also involves logistical, financial, and legal considerations. By addressing these challenges and capitalizing on the opportunities of a diverse global workforce, organizations can enhance innovation, competitiveness, and overall success in the global market.

Human Capital Theory underscores the significance of investing in human resources to enhance individual and organizational performance. By applying the principles of this theory, organizations can optimize their workforce, achieve sustainable growth, and maintain a competitive advantage in the market. Despite challenges, the continued evolution of Human Capital Theory holds promise for more accurate measurement and effective management of an organization's most valuable asset—its people.

CHAPTER SIX

COST AND VALUATION APPROACHES

Introduction to Cost and Valuation Approaches

Cost and valuation approaches in Human Resource Accounting (HRA) serve as essential methods for quantifying the economic value of human resources. These approaches offer organizations the means to evaluate their investments in employees, encompassing aspects such as recruitment, training, and development, as well as the potential returns from employees' performance and productivity. By utilizing cost approaches, organizations can analyze various expenses related to human resources, helping to identify inefficiencies and areas for optimization. Valuation approaches, on the other hand, focus on projecting the future economic benefits derived from employees, enabling organizations to make informed decisions about resource allocation and strategic planning. Together, these approaches provide a comprehensive framework for understanding the financial impact of human capital and aligning HR practices with organizational goals for sustained growth and success.

Cost-Based Approaches

Cost-based approaches in Human Resource Accounting (HRA) primarily emphasize the historical costs involved in acquiring, developing, and maintaining human resources. These approaches provide a structured method to quantify the investments made in employees. Here are some common cost-based approaches:

Acquisition Cost Method: The Acquisition Cost Method calculates the expenses incurred during the recruiting, hiring, and onboarding processes for new employees. This method provides a comprehensive view of the financial investment required to attract and integrate new talent into an organization. Key components of this method include advertising costs for job postings on various platforms, fees paid to recruitment agencies for their services, interview-related expenses such as candidate travel and accommodation, and relocation costs for new hires who need to move to a different location. Additionally, it encompasses onboarding costs, including initial orientation and training programs to help new employees acclimate to their roles. By quantifying these expenses, organizations can better understand the financial impact of their hiring practices and make informed decisions to optimize their recruitment strategies and resource allocation.

Training and Development Cost Method: The Training and Development Cost Method focuses on quantifying the expenses incurred in enhancing employees' skills and capabilities. This approach encompasses a wide range of costs associated with various training and development activities. It includes expenses for organizing and conducting training programs, workshops, and seminars aimed at improving specific skills or knowledge areas. Additionally, it covers the costs of enrolling employees in professional development courses, obtaining certifications, and attending industry conferences. These investments are crucial for maintaining a competitive and competent workforce, as they ensure that employees stay updated with the latest industry trends and best practices. By measuring these costs, organizations can assess the effectiveness of their training initiatives and make informed decisions about resource allocation to optimize employee development and overall performance.

Replacement Cost Method: The Replacement Cost Method estimates the financial impact of replacing an employee with a similar level of skills and experience. This method accounts for several factors, including the costs of recruitment and selection, such as advertising, agency fees, and interview expenses. It also considers the training and onboarding expenses required to bring the new hire up to the productivity level of the departing employee. Additionally, the method includes the cost of lost productivity during the transition period, when the organization may experience reduced efficiency and potential disruptions. By evaluating these components, the Replacement Cost Method provides a comprehensive view of the investment needed to replace an employee, helping organizations make informed decisions about workforce management and planning.

Opportunity Cost Method: The Opportunity Cost Method evaluates the potential benefits that are lost when an employee departs from an organization. This approach considers the value of foregone opportunities that could have been achieved if the employee had remained. It includes the costs associated with reduced productivity during the period when the position is vacant or when a new hire is being integrated into the team. Additionally, the Opportunity Cost Method takes into account the impact on team dynamics, such as disruptions in workflow, increased workload for remaining team members, and potential delays in project timelines. By assessing these factors, organizations can gain a comprehensive understanding of the broader economic implications of employee turnover and make more informed decisions to minimize these costs and enhance workforce stability.

Value-Based Approaches

Value-based approaches in Human Resource Accounting focus on determining the present value of future economic benefits generated by human resources. These approaches aim to quantify the long-term contributions of employees to the organization. Common value-based approaches include the Earnings Approach, which calculates the present value of future earnings attributable to employees based on their expected tenure and performance. The Market Value Approach estimates the value of human resources by comparing them to similar assets or workforce data in the market. The Income Approach evaluates the potential income generated by employees over their productive years, discounted to present value. These methods provide valuable insights into the economic impact of human capital, aiding organizations in strategic planning, resource allocation, and optimizing workforce investments for sustained growth and success. Some common value-based approaches include:

Present Value of Future Earnings Method: The Present Value of Future Earnings Method projects the future earnings of employees and then discounts them to their present value, offering a comprehensive evaluation of the economic benefits employees will generate over time. This method takes into account various factors, including employee performance, productivity, and their potential for future growth and career advancement within the organization. By analyzing these elements, organizations can estimate the value of an employee's future contributions and assess the return on investment in human capital. This approach provides valuable insights for strategic workforce planning, helping organizations make informed decisions about training, development, and retention initiatives that align with their long-term goals and optimize their human capital investments.

Economic Value Added (EVA) Method: The Economic Value Added (EVA) Method is a value-based approach that measures the value created by employees beyond their cost to the organization. This method calculates the economic profit generated by human resources after accounting for the cost of capital. Essentially, it assesses whether the returns produced by employees exceed the company's cost of investing in them. By evaluating factors such as employee performance, productivity, and their contributions to revenue and profit growth, the EVA Method provides a comprehensive view of the economic impact of human capital. This approach helps organizations determine the true value added by their workforce, guiding strategic decisions related to investment in training, development, and talent management to maximize overall profitability and shareholder value.

Human Asset Multiplier Method: The Human Asset Multiplier Method estimates the value of human resources by applying a multiplier to assess their contribution to the organization's revenue and profitability. This multiplier is determined by key factors such as employee performance, experience, and skills. By considering these elements, organizations can gauge the impact of their workforce on financial outcomes more accurately. For instance, employees with higher performance ratings, extensive experience, and advanced skills are assigned a higher multiplier, reflecting their greater contribution to the company's success. This method provides a structured approach to valuing human capital, helping organizations make informed decisions about talent management, compensation, and development initiatives to maximize their workforce's overall economic value and drive long-term growth.

Comparative Analysis of Cost and Value-Based Approaches

Cost-Based Approaches:

Advantages:

- Provide a straightforward and tangible measure of investment in human resources.
- Useful for budgeting and financial planning.

Disadvantages:

- Do not capture the full economic value of human resources.

- May overlook the long-term benefits of employee development and retention.

Value-Based Approaches:
Advantages:

- Offer a comprehensive view of the economic benefits generated by human resources.
- Support strategic planning and performance evaluation.

Disadvantages:

- Involve subjective estimates and projections.
- May be complex and time-consuming to implement.

Challenges in Applying Cost and Valuation Approaches

- **Data Availability:** Accurate and comprehensive data on employee performance, skills, and potential is often challenging to obtain and measure, which poses a significant obstacle in applying cost and valuation approaches in Human Resource Accounting. The difficulty stems from the intangible nature of many aspects of human capital, such as soft skills, employee engagement, and potential for future growth. Additionally, inconsistent data collection methods, lack of standardized metrics, and variations in performance evaluation criteria can further complicate the process. Without reliable and precise data, organizations may struggle to make informed decisions about investments in human capital, leading to suboptimal resource allocation and missed opportunities for enhancing workforce productivity and development. Therefore, improving data availability and measurement techniques is crucial for accurately assessing the economic value of human resources.
- **Subjectivity:** Valuation approaches in Human Resource Accounting often involve subjective estimates, which can introduce inconsistencies in measurement and reporting. These estimates rely on assumptions about factors such as employee performance, potential, and future contributions, which can vary significantly between evaluators. The lack of standardized criteria and the inherent uncertainty in predicting future outcomes can result in different interpretations and valuations for the

same employee. This subjectivity can complicate comparisons across employees and departments, potentially leading to biased or inaccurate assessments. To mitigate these challenges, organizations must strive for greater consistency by developing clear guidelines, employing multiple evaluators, and using a combination of quantitative and qualitative data to support their valuation processes.

- **Standardization:** The lack of standardized methods and practices for cost and valuation approaches in Human Resource Accounting can lead to significant variations in how organizations measure and report human capital. Without a consistent framework, companies may adopt different criteria and metrics, resulting in inconsistent and incomparable data across the industry. This lack of standardization can hinder the ability to benchmark performance, assess the true value of human resources, and make informed strategic decisions. Additionally, it complicates external reporting and transparency, as stakeholders may struggle to interpret and trust the information provided. To address these challenges, developing and implementing standardized methodologies and practices is crucial, enabling more accurate, reliable, and comparable assessments of human capital across organizations.

- **Cost and Complexity:** Implementing cost and valuation approaches in Human Resource Accounting necessitates a significant investment in data collection, analysis, and reporting, posing challenges for many organizations. These approaches require extensive and accurate data on various aspects of human capital, including employee performance, skills, and development activities. Gathering such data often involves sophisticated HR information systems, regular monitoring, and comprehensive record-keeping, all of which demand substantial financial and human resources. Additionally, analyzing this data to derive meaningful insights requires advanced analytical tools and expertise, further adding to the complexity and cost. For smaller organizations or those with limited resources, these challenges can be particularly daunting, potentially leading to incomplete or inaccurate assessments of human capital value. Consequently, organizations must carefully weigh the benefits against the costs and complexities when considering the implementation of these approaches, ensuring they have the necessary infrastructure and capabilities to support them effectively.

Case Studies and Examples

- **Infosys Limited:** Infosys uses the present value of future earnings method to quantify its human resources. This approach allows the company to project the future economic benefits generated by its employees and incorporate these values into its financial statements.
- **Tata Consultancy Services (TCS):** TCS employs the replacement cost method to estimate the cost of replacing employees with similar skills and experience. This approach helps the company understand the financial impact of employee turnover and make informed decisions about retention strategies.

Conclusion

Cost and valuation approaches in Human Resource Accounting provide valuable methods for measuring and quantifying the economic value of human resources. By applying these approaches, organizations can gain insights into their investment in human capital and make informed decisions about resource allocation, strategic planning, and performance evaluation. Despite challenges, the continued development and application of cost and valuation approaches hold promise for more accurate and comprehensive measurement and reporting of an organization's most valuable asset—its people.

CHAPTER SEVEN

ECONOMIC VALUE ADDED (EVA)

Introduction to Economic Value Added (EVA)

Economic Value Added (EVA) is a financial performance measure that calculates the value created by a company beyond its cost of capital. It was developed by the consulting firm Stern Stewart & Co. in the 1980s and has since gained popularity as a tool for assessing value creation and profitability. EVA is particularly useful in Human Resource Accounting (HRA) for evaluating the contributions of human capital to an organization's economic performance.

Key Principles of EVA

- **Net Operating Profit After Taxes (NOPAT):** Net Operating Profit After Taxes (NOPAT) is a key financial metric used in the calculation of Economic Value Added (EVA). NOPAT represents the operating profit of a company after making necessary adjustments for taxes, thereby providing a clear and accurate picture of the company's core operating performance. Unlike net income, which may be influenced by various non-operating factors such as interest income, extraordinary items, and tax strategies, NOPAT focuses solely on the profit generated from the company's primary business activities. This makes it a more reliable indicator of the company's operational efficiency and profitability. By using NOPAT as the starting point for EVA, organizations can better assess the true economic value created by their operations, helping them make informed decisions about resource allocation, investment opportunities, and overall financial strategy.

- **Capital Employed:** Capital Employed refers to the total capital investment in a company, encompassing both equity and debt. It represents the financial resources that a company utilizes to generate profits and sustain its operations. Capital Employed is calculated by adding shareholders' equity and long-term liabilities, providing a comprehensive view of the funds that are actively invested in the business. This metric is crucial for evaluating the efficiency and effectiveness with which a company uses its capital to generate returns. By analyzing Capital Employed, stakeholders can assess the company's financial health, operational performance, and overall ability to create value through its core activities. It also helps in comparing the profitability and capital utilization of different companies within the same industry.

- **Cost of Capital:** The cost of capital represents the weighted average cost of equity and debt that a company utilizes to finance its operations. This metric reflects the minimum return that investors and creditors expect in exchange for providing financial resources to the company. The cost of equity is the return that shareholders require for their investment, often influenced by the company's risk profile and growth prospects. The cost of debt is the interest rate that the company pays on its borrowed funds, adjusted for tax benefits. By combining these two components, the weighted average cost of capital (WACC) provides a comprehensive measure of the overall cost of financing. It serves as a critical benchmark for evaluating investment opportunities, as projects must generate returns above the WACC to create value for shareholders. Understanding the cost of capital helps organizations make informed decisions about capital structure, resource allocation, and long-term financial planning.

- **Economic Value Added (EVA) Calculation:** Economic Value Added (EVA) is a financial performance metric that measures the value created by a company beyond the required return of its shareholders. The calculation of EVA involves subtracting the cost of capital from Net Operating Profit After Taxes (NOPAT). The formula for EVA is as follows:

  $$EVA = NOPAT - (Capital\ Employed \times WACC)$$

This calculation determines the value created by the company above and beyond the cost of capital.

Application of EVA in Human Resource Accounting

- **Assessing Human Capital Contribution:** Economic Value Added (EVA) is a powerful tool for evaluating the contributions of human capital to an organization's economic performance. By incorporating the costs and benefits associated with human resources, companies can gain a clearer understanding of the value their workforce creates. This assessment involves analyzing various factors such as recruitment, training, compensation, and productivity to determine the overall financial impact of human capital. By comparing the costs of investing in employees to the economic value they generate, organizations can identify areas where their workforce is creating significant value and areas that may require improvement or additional investment. This holistic approach enables companies to make more informed decisions about talent management, optimize resource allocation, and ultimately enhance their overall performance and competitiveness in the market. Through regular assessment and continuous improvement, organizations can ensure that their human capital remains a key driver of long-term success.

- **Performance Measurement:** Economic Value Added (EVA) offers a comprehensive measure of financial performance by considering both operating profits and the cost of capital. This metric enables organizations to evaluate the true economic profit generated by their operations after accounting for the expenses of funding those operations. By incorporating EVA into performance measurement, companies can gain a clearer understanding of the value created by their human resource policies and practices. This includes assessing the impact of recruitment, training, development, and employee retention strategies on overall profitability. EVA helps identify areas where investments in human capital are yielding substantial returns and areas that may require adjustments or improvements. By regularly monitoring EVA, organizations can ensure their HR initiatives are aligned with their financial goals, fostering a culture of continuous improvement and value creation.

- **Incentive Compensation:** Economic Value Added (EVA) can be effectively used as a basis for designing incentive compensation programs. By linking employee rewards to the value they help create, organizations can align the interests of employees with those of shareholders. This alignment fosters a culture of accountability and performance improvement, as employees are motivated to focus on activities that enhance the company's overall economic value.

Using EVA as a performance metric in incentive compensation programs ensures that rewards are tied to meaningful financial outcomes, beyond traditional profit measures. It encourages employees to consider the cost of capital in their decision-making processes, promoting more efficient use of resources and a greater focus on long-term value creation. By rewarding employees based on EVA, organizations can drive behaviors that lead to sustainable growth, higher profitability, and improved shareholder returns. This approach not only incentivizes individual performance but also fosters a collective effort towards achieving the company's strategic objectives, ultimately benefiting all stakeholders.

- **Strategic Decision-Making:** Economic Value Added (EVA) offers valuable insights that aid organizations in making informed strategic decisions. By incorporating EVA into the decision-making process, companies can identify key areas for investment that are likely to yield positive returns, thereby driving sustainable growth. EVA highlights opportunities for cost reduction by pinpointing inefficiencies and areas where resources are not being utilized optimally. Additionally, it enables organizations to assess the performance of various business units, products, or projects, guiding them in reallocating resources to areas that generate the most value. This comprehensive approach ensures that strategic decisions are aligned with the goal of maximizing economic profit and enhancing overall financial performance, ultimately leading to a stronger competitive position in the market.

Benefits of Using EVA

- **Focus on Value Creation:** Economic Value Added (EVA) emphasizes value creation beyond just covering the cost of capital, pushing organizations to concentrate on profitable growth and efficient resource utilization. By measuring the true economic profit after accounting for the cost of capital, EVA helps identify activities and projects that genuinely add value to the company. This focus encourages organizations to optimize their operations, streamline processes, and invest in initiatives that generate substantial returns. By prioritizing value creation, companies can ensure sustainable growth, enhance competitiveness, and drive long-term success. EVA also promotes a culture of accountability and performance excellence, as employees and management are aligned towards achieving financial objectives that benefit both the company and its stakeholders.

- **Alignment of Interests:** By linking employee compensation to Economic Value Added (EVA), organizations create a powerful alignment of interests between employees, management, and shareholders. This approach ensures that everyone is working towards the common goal of maximizing economic profit and long-term value creation. When employees' rewards are directly tied to EVA, they are incentivized to focus on activities and projects that generate substantial returns and drive efficient use of resources. This fosters a culture of performance and accountability, as employees and management are motivated to make decisions that enhance the company's overall financial health. By aligning their interests with those of shareholders, organizations can create a cohesive and motivated workforce dedicated to achieving strategic objectives and sustaining profitable growth.

- **Comprehensive Performance Measure:** Economic Value Added (EVA) serves as a holistic and robust measure of financial performance, as it accounts for both operating profits and the cost of capital. Unlike traditional financial metrics that may focus solely on earnings or profits, EVA provides a more complete assessment by considering the capital costs required to generate those profits. This approach ensures that the true economic value created by the organization is accurately measured, offering a clear and precise picture of its overall economic performance. By integrating EVA into performance measurement, organizations can better understand the effectiveness of their business strategies, identify value-generating activities, and make informed decisions to drive sustainable growth and profitability. It also enhances transparency and accountability, as stakeholders gain a comprehensive view of the company's financial health and value creation efforts.

- **Improved Decision-Making:** Economic Value Added (EVA) enhances decision-making by offering valuable insights into the financial impact of strategic initiatives and investments. By analyzing EVA, organizations can assess whether proposed projects and strategies will generate returns that exceed the cost of capital, ensuring that only value-creating initiatives are pursued. This comprehensive approach allows companies to evaluate the true economic benefits and risks associated with different options, facilitating more informed and effective choices. EVA also highlights areas where resources can be reallocated to maximize value, promoting efficient use of capital and driving sustainable growth. By incorporating EVA into their decision-making processes, organizations can align their strategic goals with long-term financial performance, ultimately enhancing overall profitability and shareholder value.

Challenges in Implementing EVA

- **Complexity:** Calculating Economic Value Added (EVA) is a multifaceted process that involves numerous steps and adjustments, contributing to its complexity. To begin with, organizations need to determine Net Operating Profit After Taxes (NOPAT), which requires accurate accounting for operating profits and tax adjustments. Additionally, calculating the cost of capital involves determining the weighted average cost of equity and debt, which can be influenced by various factors such as market conditions, interest rates, and the company's risk profile. Furthermore, adjustments may be necessary to account for non-operating items, extraordinary expenses, and other financial anomalies that could distort the true economic value generated by the company. The intricate nature of these calculations demands a thorough understanding of financial principles, precise data collection, and sophisticated analytical tools. As a result, implementing and comprehending EVA can be challenging for organizations, requiring specialized knowledge and expertise to ensure accurate and meaningful results.

- **Data Availability:** Accurate and comprehensive data on operating profits, capital employed, and the cost of capital are essential for calculating Economic Value Added (EVA). However, obtaining this data can be challenging for some organizations. This difficulty arises due to several factors, including the complexity of financial reporting systems, the need for precise and up-to-date financial records, and the variations in data collection practices across different departments. Additionally, certain non-operating items, extraordinary expenses, and adjustments for tax and capital costs require meticulous tracking and documentation. For smaller organizations or those with limited resources, maintaining such detailed financial records can be particularly burdensome. The lack of standardized data collection methods and the need for sophisticated analytical tools further exacerbate the challenge. Ensuring data accuracy and completeness is crucial for meaningful EVA calculations, as any discrepancies or omissions can lead to inaccurate assessments and suboptimal decision-making. Therefore, organizations must invest in robust financial management systems and practices to overcome these challenges and derive reliable insights from EVA.

- **Subjectivity:** Economic Value Added (EVA) calculations often involve subjective estimates and assumptions, which can impact the accuracy and reliability of this measure. These subjectivities arise from various factors, including forecasts of future earnings, determination of the appropriate cost of capital, and adjustments for non-operating items. For instance, estimating future earnings involves predicting market conditions, employee performance, and other dynamic variables that can be highly uncertain. Similarly, determining the weighted average cost of capital (WACC) requires assumptions about the cost of equity and debt, which can be influenced by market volatility and changes in investor expectations. Furthermore, the need to adjust for extraordinary items, non-operating expenses, and other financial anomalies requires judgment calls that can vary between evaluators. These subjective elements can lead to inconsistencies in EVA calculations, making it challenging to compare results across different periods or organizations. To mitigate these challenges, organizations must adopt clear guidelines, use standardized assumptions where possible, and combine quantitative data with expert judgment to enhance the reliability and comparability of EVA assessments.

- **Cost:** Implementing Economic Value Added (EVA) necessitates a substantial investment in data collection, analysis, and reporting, which can be particularly challenging for smaller organizations. The process requires detailed and accurate financial records, sophisticated information systems, and advanced analytical tools to ensure precise calculations. Collecting comprehensive data on operating profits, capital employed, and the cost of capital involves continuous monitoring and meticulous record-keeping. Additionally, the need for specialized expertise to interpret and analyze this data further adds to the costs. For smaller organizations with limited financial and human resources, these requirements can be burdensome, potentially hindering their ability to fully leverage EVA as a performance measure. To overcome these challenges, smaller organizations may need to prioritize building robust financial management systems and investing in training and development to enhance their capabilities in EVA implementation. Balancing the costs against the potential benefits of improved decision-making and value creation is essential for making informed choices about adopting EVA.

Case Studies and Examples

- **Infosys Limited:** Infosys uses EVA as part of its performance measurement and incentive compensation programs. By linking employee rewards to EVA, the company encourages value creation and aligns employee interests with shareholder interests.
- **Tata Consultancy Services (TCS):** TCS employs EVA to assess the financial performance of its business units and make strategic decisions. The company uses EVA to identify areas for investment, cost reduction, and performance improvement.

Future Trends in EVA

- **Integration with Technology:** The use of advanced technologies, such as artificial intelligence and big data analytics, to improve the accuracy and efficiency of EVA calculations and reporting.
- **Sustainability and CSR Initiatives:** Integrating EVA into broader sustainability and corporate social responsibility initiatives to reflect the true value of an organization's economic performance.
- **Global Adoption:** Increasing global adoption of EVA as a standard measure of financial performance, driven by its comprehensive and value-focused approach.

Conclusion

Economic Value Added (EVA) is a powerful financial performance measure that calculates the value created by a company beyond its cost of capital. By applying EVA in Human Resource Accounting, organizations can assess the contributions of human capital, improve performance measurement, and support strategic decision-making. Despite challenges, the benefits of EVA make it a valuable tool for modern organizations committed to value creation and sustainable growth.

CHAPTER EIGHT

MEASUREMENT AND VALUATION

Introduction to Measurement and Valuation

Measurement and valuation are critical components of Human Resource Accounting (HRA). They provide the methods and frameworks for quantifying the value of human resources and incorporating this value into financial statements. Accurate measurement and valuation enable organizations to make informed decisions about investments in human capital, performance evaluation, and strategic planning.

Measurement Approaches in HRA

- **Historical Cost Approach:** The Historical Cost Approach involves recording and accounting for the actual costs incurred in acquiring, developing, and maintaining employees. This method includes various expenses such as recruitment, training, compensation, benefits, and other related costs. By focusing on the historical costs, organizations can obtain a straightforward and tangible measure of their investment in human resources. This approach provides a clear picture of the financial resources allocated to building and sustaining the workforce, allowing organizations to track and manage their expenditures effectively. Additionally, it offers valuable insights into the cost-effectiveness of HR practices and helps in budgeting and financial planning. However, it's important to note that the Historical Cost Approach does not capture the future potential and value of employees, as it is primarily concerned with past expenditures. Nonetheless, it remains a fundamental method for understanding and managing the financial aspects of human capital investment.

- **Replacement Cost Approach:** The Replacement Cost Approach estimates the cost of replacing an employee with similar skills and experience, providing a clear view of the financial impact of employee turnover. This method considers various factors, including recruitment costs, training expenses, and the productivity lost during the transition period when a new employee is being onboarded and acclimated to the role. By assessing these costs, organizations can gauge the economic implications of losing a valuable employee and understand the resources required to bring a new hire up to the same level of proficiency. This approach emphasizes the importance of employee retention strategies and effective talent management, as high turnover rates can lead to significant financial burdens. By highlighting the true cost of replacement, organizations can make more informed decisions about investing in employee development and retention programs, ultimately fostering a more stable and productive workforce.

- **Opportunity Cost Approach:** The Opportunity Cost Approach assesses the potential benefits lost when an employee departs from the organization, offering a comprehensive view of the financial and operational impact of employee turnover. This method considers the costs associated with lost opportunities, such as unachieved business goals, missed sales, or delayed projects, that result from the absence of a key employee. Additionally, it takes into account the reduced productivity that occurs during the transition period, as remaining team members may need to pick up extra responsibilities or new hires take time to reach full efficiency. The impact on team dynamics is also a critical factor, as losing a valuable employee can disrupt collaboration, morale, and overall team performance. By highlighting these opportunity costs, organizations can better understand the true value of retaining their employees and the importance of implementing effective retention strategies. This approach underscores the need for proactive talent management and employee engagement initiatives to minimize turnover and maintain a stable, productive workforce.

Valuation Approaches in HRA

- **Present Value of Future Earnings Method:** This method estimates the future earnings potential of employees and discounts these projected earnings to present value, providing a comprehensive view of the economic benefits generated by human resources. It involves forecasting the expected future income that an employee will generate for the organization, considering factors such as their performance, productivity, and potential for growth. These future earnings are then discounted using an appropriate discount rate to reflect their present value, accounting for the time value of money. This approach helps organizations assess the long-term financial contributions of their employees, enabling them to make informed decisions about talent management, development, and retention strategies. By quantifying the present value of future earnings, companies can better understand the economic impact of their workforce and allocate resources more effectively to maximize overall profitability and growth.

- **Economic Value Added (EVA) Method:** The EVA method measures the value created by employees beyond their cost to the organization by calculating the economic profit generated by human resources after accounting for the cost of capital. This approach emphasizes value creation and the efficient use of resources, aligning employee performance with the overall financial goals of the organization. By focusing on the economic profit generated by employees, the EVA method provides a clear and objective measure of the contributions made by human capital to the company's success. EVA is calculated using the following formula:

    - EVA=NOPAT−(Capital Employed×WACC)
    - **Where:**
      NOPAT (Net Operating Profit After Taxes) represents the operating profit after accounting for taxes.
      Capital Employed refers to the total capital investment in the company, including both equity and debt.
      WACC (Weighted Average Cost of Capital) is the average rate of return required by all of the company's investors, both equity and debt holders.
      By incorporating the cost of capital into the assessment, EVA ensures that only those activities and investments that generate returns above the cost of capital are considered value-creating. This method encourages organizations to focus on profitable growth, efficient resource utilization, and strategic decision-making that enhances overall economic value. EVA also serves as a basis for

performance measurement, incentive compensation, and strategic planning, helping organizations align their human resource policies and practices with their financial objectives to drive long-term success.

- **Human Asset Multiplier Method:** This method uses a multiplier to estimate the value of human resources based on their contribution to the organization's revenue and profitability. The multiplier is determined by factors such as employee performance, experience, and skills. By assigning a numerical value or coefficient to these factors, the Human Asset Multiplier Method provides a practical approach to quantifying human capital. This method involves evaluating employees' impact on various performance metrics, such as sales, productivity, and customer satisfaction, and then applying the multiplier to determine their overall value to the organization. This approach enables companies to recognize and reward the contributions of high-performing employees, identify areas for improvement, and make informed decisions about talent management and resource allocation. By integrating both qualitative and quantitative aspects, the Human Asset Multiplier Method offers a balanced and comprehensive view of the economic significance of human resources.

Steps in Measuring and Valuing Human Resources

- **Data Collection:** Gathering accurate and comprehensive data on employee performance, skills, compensation, and potential is crucial for effectively measuring and valuing human resources. This data serves as the foundation for various valuation methods, ensuring that assessments are based on reliable and detailed information.
- **Selection of Measurement and Valuation Methods:** It is essential to choose the appropriate methods for measuring and valuing human resources based on the organization's specific objectives, available data, and overall context. This selection process should consider both cost-based and value-based approaches to provide a comprehensive view of human resource value. Cost-based approaches focus on the expenses associated with acquiring, developing, and maintaining employees, such as recruitment, training, and compensation. These methods offer tangible and straightforward measures of investment in human capital.

On the other hand, value-based approaches assess the economic contributions of employees, considering their impact on revenue, profitability, and long-term growth. Methods like the Economic Value Added (EVA) method, Present Value of Future Earnings, and Human Asset Multiplier provide insights into the value created by human resources beyond their costs. By integrating both cost-based and value-based perspectives, organizations can gain a holistic understanding of their human capital's financial and strategic significance, enabling informed decision-making and effective talent management.

- **Calculation and Analysis:** After selecting the appropriate methods for measuring and valuing human resources, the next step is to perform calculations to quantify their value. This involves applying the chosen cost-based and value-based approaches to the collected data on employee performance, skills, compensation, and potential. By systematically calculating metrics such as the cost of recruitment, training, and compensation, as well as the economic contributions of employees, organizations can obtain a comprehensive measure of their human capital investment.

  Once the calculations are complete, it is crucial to analyze the results to gain insights into the impact of human capital on organizational performance. This analysis involves examining the financial and strategic significance of human resources, identifying areas where investments in employees have yielded substantial returns, and pinpointing opportunities for improvement. By understanding the value generated by human capital, organizations can make informed decisions about resource allocation, talent management, and strategic planning. This comprehensive approach enables companies to optimize their workforce, enhance productivity, and drive long-term success.

- **Reporting and Communication:** Incorporating the measured and valued human resource data into financial statements and reports is a crucial step in enhancing transparency and informing decision-making. By integrating human capital metrics into financial disclosures, organizations can provide stakeholders with a comprehensive view of the value generated by their workforce. This includes detailed information on employee performance, skills, compensation, and potential, as well as the financial impact of human capital investments.

  Effectively communicating these findings to stakeholders, such as investors, board members, and employees, helps build trust and ensures that everyone is aligned with the organization's strategic goals. Clear and transparent reporting enables stakeholders to understand the contributions of human resources to overall organizational performance, identify areas for improvement, and make informed decisions about future investments and initiatives. By prioritizing reporting and communication, organizations can foster a culture of accountability, continuous improvement, and long-term value creation.

Challenges in Measurement and Valuation

- **Data Availability:** Accurate and comprehensive data on employee performance, skills, and potential can be difficult to obtain and measure.
- **Subjectivity:** Valuation approaches involve subjective estimates and projections, which can lead to inconsistencies in measurement and reporting.
- **Standardization:** The lack of standardized methods and practices for measurement and valuation can result in variations in how organizations quantify human capital.
- **Cost and Complexity:** Implementing measurement and valuation approaches requires significant investment in data collection, analysis, and reporting, which can be challenging for some organizations.

Case Studies and Examples

- **Infosys Limited:** Infosys employs the present value of future earnings method to quantify its human resources. This approach allows the company to project the future economic benefits generated by its employees and incorporate these values into its financial statements.
- **Tata Consultancy Services (TCS):** TCS uses the replacement cost method to estimate the cost of replacing employees with similar skills and experience. This approach helps the company understand the financial impact of employee turnover and make informed decisions about retention strategies.

Conclusion

Measurement and valuation are essential for recognizing and quantifying the value of human resources in Human Resource Accounting. By applying appropriate methods and approaches, organizations can gain insights into their investment in human capital and make informed decisions about resource allocation, strategic planning, and performance evaluation. Despite challenges, the continued development and application of measurement and valuation practices hold promise for more accurate and comprehensive reporting of an organization's most valuable asset—its people.

CHAPTER NINE

Cost-Based Methods

Introduction to Cost-Based Methods

Cost-based methods in Human Resource Accounting (HRA) focus on quantifying the historical costs associated with acquiring, developing, and maintaining human resources. These methods provide tangible measures of the financial investment made in employees and help organizations understand the cost implications of their human resource practices.

Key Cost-Based Methods

Acquisition Cost Method

The Acquisition Cost Method focuses on calculating the expenses incurred in the process of recruiting, hiring, and onboarding employees. This approach encompasses a range of costs, including advertising expenses for job postings, fees paid to recruitment agencies, expenses related to conducting interviews (such as travel and accommodation for candidates), and relocation costs for new hires. By accurately tracking and recording these expenditures, organizations can gain a clear understanding of the financial investment required to acquire new talent. This method provides valuable insights into the cost-effectiveness of recruitment strategies and helps in budgeting and financial planning. By analyzing acquisition costs, companies can identify areas where they can optimize their recruitment processes, reduce expenses, and improve overall efficiency in attracting and onboarding new employees.

Training and Development Cost Method: This method measures the expenses associated with training and developing employees. It encompasses a wide range of costs, including those for training programs, workshops, seminars, professional development courses, and on-the-job training. By tracking these expenditures, organizations can understand the financial investment required to enhance employees' skills and knowledge.

This method underscores the importance of investing in human capital, as well-trained and knowledgeable employees contribute significantly to improved performance and productivity. Additionally, it highlights the benefits of continuous learning and development in fostering a skilled and competent workforce, ultimately driving organizational success and competitive advantage.

Replacement Cost Method: This method focuses on estimating the cost of replacing an employee with a similar level of skills and experience. It takes into account various factors such as recruitment expenses, training costs, and the productivity lost during the transition period. The process includes advertising job openings, interviewing candidates, and onboarding new hires. Additionally, the costs of training new employees to reach the same level of proficiency as their predecessors are considered. The replacement cost method provides valuable insights into the financial impact of employee turnover, emphasizing the importance of effective retention strategies. By understanding these costs, organizations can better appreciate the value of retaining skilled employees and invest in programs that enhance employee satisfaction and loyalty, ultimately reducing turnover and its associated expenses.

Opportunity Cost Method: This approach evaluates the potential benefits lost when an employee departs from the organization. It takes into account various elements, such as the cost of lost opportunities, reduced productivity, and the disruption to team dynamics. When a valuable employee leaves, the organization may miss out on potential sales, delayed projects, and unachieved business goals. Additionally, the productivity of the remaining team members can decline as they pick up additional responsibilities or await the onboarding of a new hire. The impact on team dynamics is significant, as the departure of a key employee can affect collaboration, morale, and overall team performance.

By assessing these opportunity costs, organizations can better understand the true financial impact of employee turnover. This method underscores the importance of retaining valuable employees and implementing effective retention strategies. By investing in employee engagement, development, and satisfaction programs, companies can reduce turnover rates and maintain a stable, productive workforce, ultimately minimizing the opportunity costs associated with losing key talent.

Steps in Applying Cost-Based Methods

- **Data Collection:** Gather accurate and comprehensive data on recruitment, training, development, and turnover costs. This data serves as the foundation for applying cost-based methods.
- **Calculation of Costs:** Use the collected data to calculate the costs associated with each method. For example, add up recruitment and hiring expenses for the acquisition cost method, or training program expenses for the training and development cost method.
- **Analysis and Interpretation:** Analyze the calculated costs to gain insights into the financial investment in human resources. Compare the costs across different departments, positions, and time periods to identify trends and areas for improvement.
- **Reporting and Communication:** Incorporate the calculated costs into financial statements and reports. Communicate the findings to stakeholders to enhance transparency and inform decision-making.

Benefits of Cost-Based Methods

- **Tangible Measures:** Cost-based methods provide tangible and quantifiable measures of the financial investment in human resources, making it easier to understand and analyze.
- **Budgeting and Financial Planning:** These methods support budgeting and financial planning by providing insights into the costs associated with human resource practices.
- **Informed Decision-Making:** Cost-based methods help organizations make informed decisions about recruitment, training, and retention strategies by highlighting the financial implications of different practices.
- **Performance Evaluation:** These methods provide a framework for evaluating the effectiveness of human resource policies and practices by measuring their cost impact.

Challenges in Applying Cost-Based Methods

- **Data Availability:** Accurate and comprehensive data on recruitment, training, and turnover costs can be difficult to obtain and measure.
- **Cost and Complexity:** Implementing cost-based methods requires significant investment in data collection, analysis, and reporting, which can be challenging for some organizations.

- **Scope and Limitations:** Cost-based methods focus on historical costs and may not capture the full economic value of human resources or the long-term benefits of employee development and retention.

Case Studies and Examples

Infosys Limited: Infosys uses the training and development cost method to measure the expenses associated with its comprehensive training programs. This approach allows the company to quantify its investment in employee development and assess the effectiveness of its training initiatives.

Tata Consultancy Services (TCS): TCS employs the replacement cost method to estimate the cost of replacing employees with similar skills and experience. This method helps the company understand the financial impact of employee turnover and make informed decisions about retention strategies.

Conclusion

Cost-based methods in Human Resource Accounting provide valuable insights into the financial investment in human resources. By applying these methods, organizations can quantify the costs associated with acquiring, developing, and maintaining employees, support budgeting and financial planning, and make informed decisions about human resource practices. Despite challenges, the benefits of cost-based methods make them a valuable tool for understanding and managing the financial implications of human resource management.

CHAPTER TEN

MARKET-BASED METHODS

Introduction to Market-Based Methods

Market-based methods in Human Resource Accounting (HRA) focus on quantifying the value of human resources based on market conditions and comparable benchmarks. These methods provide insights into how human resources are valued in the marketplace and help organizations assess the competitive positioning of their workforce.

Key Market-Based Methods

Comparative Market Value Method

This method involves comparing the value of an organization's human resources with similar positions in the market. It uses market salary surveys and industry benchmarks to determine the market value of employees' skills and experiences. By leveraging data from these surveys and benchmarks, organizations can gain insights into prevailing compensation trends, ensuring that their pay structures remain competitive. This approach helps companies understand how their compensation packages compare to industry standards and identify any disparities that may exist. By aligning their compensation practices with market rates, organizations can attract and retain top talent, foster employee satisfaction, and enhance overall workforce performance. Additionally, the Comparative Market Value Method provides a basis for making informed decisions about salary adjustments, promotions, and employee benefits, promoting fairness and equity within the organization.

Human Resource Valuation through Mergers and Acquisitions (M&A)

In the context of mergers and acquisitions, human resource valuation plays a pivotal role during the due diligence process. This assessment focuses on determining the market value of the acquired workforce by considering various factors such as employees' skills, experience, and their potential contributions to the merged entity. By evaluating these aspects, organizations can accurately gauge the overall worth of the acquisition. Additionally, this valuation aids in shaping negotiation strategies and ensuring a smooth integration of the workforce, ultimately contributing to the success of the merged entity.

Replacement Cost Method

The replacement cost method, though primarily a cost-based approach, can also be aligned with market-based valuation techniques. This method involves estimating the expenses associated with replacing an existing employee with a new hire who possesses comparable skills and experience. It takes into account the current market conditions, recruitment costs, and prevailing salary levels for similar positions. By considering these factors, organizations can effectively determine the financial impact of losing and subsequently replacing an employee. This approach is particularly useful in assessing the value of human capital during mergers and acquisitions, as it provides a realistic estimate of the investment required to maintain the workforce's competency and productivity levels.

Steps in Applying Market-Based Methods

- **Data Collection:** Gather market data on compensation, benefits, and other relevant benchmarks for similar positions in the industry. This data can be obtained from salary surveys, industry reports, and professional associations.
- **Benchmarking:** Compare the organization's human resource values with market data to identify disparities and areas for alignment. Analyze how the organization's compensation packages, benefits, and development opportunities compare to market standards.
- **Valuation and Adjustment:** Use the collected data to value human resources based on market conditions. Make necessary adjustments to compensation packages, benefits, and human resource policies to align with market benchmarks and remain competitive.
- **Reporting and Communication:** Incorporate the market-based valuation data into financial statements and reports. Communicate the findings to stakeholders to enhance transparency and support informed decision-making.

Benefits of Market-Based Methods

- **Competitive Positioning:** Market-based methods help organizations understand their competitive positioning in terms of compensation and benefits, enabling them to attract and retain top talent.
- **Informed Decision-Making:** These methods provide insights into market trends and benchmarks, supporting informed decisions about human resource practices and strategies.
- **Alignment with Market Standards:** By benchmarking against market data, organizations can ensure their compensation packages and human resource policies are aligned with industry standards.
- **Enhanced Transparency:** Market-based methods enhance transparency by providing stakeholders with a clear understanding of how human resources are valued in the marketplace.

Challenges in Applying Market-Based Methods

- **Data Availability:** Obtaining accurate and comprehensive market data on compensation and benefits can be challenging, particularly for specialized or niche positions.
- **Market Fluctuations:** Market conditions can change rapidly, affecting the accuracy and relevance of the valuation data. Organizations must continuously update their market-based valuations to reflect current trends.
- **Cost and Complexity:** Implementing market-based methods requires significant investment in data collection, analysis, and reporting, which can be resource-intensive.

Case Studies and Examples

- **Infosys Limited:** Infosys uses comparative market value methods to benchmark its compensation packages against industry standards. This approach helps the company remain competitive in attracting and retaining top talent.
- **Tata Consultancy Services (TCS):** TCS employs market-based valuation during mergers and acquisitions to assess the value of the acquired workforce. This method informs negotiation strategies and ensures the company makes informed decisions about the acquisition.

Conclusion

Market-based methods in Human Resource Accounting provide valuable insights into the value of human resources based on market conditions and benchmarks. By applying these methods, organizations can assess their competitive positioning, make informed decisions about compensation and human resource practices, and enhance transparency. Despite challenges, the benefits of market-based methods make them a valuable tool for understanding and managing the value of human resources in a dynamic marketplace.

CHAPTER ELEVEN

INCOME-BASED METHODS

Introduction to Income-Based Methods

Income-based methods in Human Resource Accounting (HRA) focus on quantifying the value of human resources based on the income or economic benefits they generate for the organization. These methods provide insights into the future earnings and contributions of employees, helping organizations assess the economic value of their workforce.

Key Income-Based Methods

Present Value of Future Earnings Method

The present value of future earnings method is a valuation approach that estimates the economic benefits generated by employees over time by projecting their future earnings and discounting them to their present value. This method takes into account various factors such as employee performance, productivity, potential for future growth, and tenure within the organization. By evaluating these aspects, organizations can gain a comprehensive understanding of the long-term value that their human resources contribute. This approach is particularly valuable in the context of mergers and acquisitions, as it helps in making informed decisions about the workforce's potential impact on the combined entity's overall performance and value.

Human Resource Valuation through Discounted Cash Flows (DCF)

Human Resource Valuation through the Discounted Cash Flow (DCF) method is a comprehensive approach that estimates the future cash flows generated by an organization's human resources and discounts them to their present value. By doing so, it provides a realistic and quantifiable measure of the workforce's long-term economic contributions. This method takes into account several critical factors, such as employee performance, productivity, potential for growth, and prevailing market conditions. Additionally, it aligns with the organization's strategic goals to ensure the accuracy of the projections. By applying the DCF method, organizations can make informed decisions regarding their workforce, especially during mergers and acquisitions, where understanding the value of human capital is crucial for negotiating and strategizing effectively.

Earnings Multipliers Method

The earnings multipliers method is a practical and efficient approach to valuing human resources by using a multiplier to estimate their contribution to an organization's revenue and profitability. This multiplier is determined by various factors, including employee performance, experience, skills, and industry benchmarks. Essentially, the method calculates the economic value of employees by correlating their ability to generate income for the organization. This method allows businesses to assess the financial impact of their human capital in a straightforward manner, making it especially useful during mergers and acquisitions where understanding the income-generating potential of the workforce is vital for accurate valuation and strategic planning. By applying this method, organizations can better appreciate the significant role that their employees play in driving profitability and sustaining growth.

Steps in Applying Income-Based Methods

- **Data Collection:** Gather accurate and comprehensive data on employee performance, productivity, compensation, and potential for future growth. This data serves as the foundation for applying income-based methods.
- **Projection of Future Earnings:** Estimate the future earnings and contributions of employees based on their current performance, potential for growth, and expected tenure within the organization.
- **Discounting to Present Value:** Use appropriate discount rates to calculate the present value of the projected future earnings. The discount rate reflects the organization's cost of capital and the risk associated with future cash flows.
- **Valuation and Analysis:** Perform the calculations to quantify the value of human resources based on the projected future earnings. Analyze the results to gain insights into the economic contributions of the workforce.

- **Reporting and Communication:** Incorporate the income-based valuation data into financial statements and reports. Communicate the findings to stakeholders to enhance transparency and inform decision-making.

Benefits of Income-Based Methods

- **Future-Oriented:** Income-based methods focus on the future economic benefits generated by human resources, providing a forward-looking perspective on their value.
- **Comprehensive View:** These methods consider various factors, including employee performance, productivity, and potential for growth, offering a holistic view of human resource value.
- **Support for Strategic Planning:** Income-based methods provide valuable insights for strategic planning, helping organizations identify areas for investment and performance improvement.
- **Enhanced Decision-Making:** By quantifying the future economic contributions of employees, income-based methods support informed decisions about resource allocation, compensation, and development.

Challenges in Applying Income-Based Methods

- **Data Availability:** Accurate and comprehensive data on employee performance, productivity, and potential for future growth can be difficult to obtain and measure.
- **Subjectivity:** Income-based methods involve subjective estimates and projections, which can lead to inconsistencies in measurement and reporting.
- **Discount Rate Selection:** Choosing an appropriate discount rate is critical for accurate valuation, but it can be challenging due to varying market conditions and organizational risk factors.
- **Cost and Complexity:** Implementing income-based methods requires significant investment in data collection, analysis, and reporting, which can be resource-intensive.

Case Studies and Examples

- **Infosys Limited:** Infosys uses the present value of future earnings method to quantify the economic value of its human resources. This approach allows the company to project the future contributions of its employees and incorporate these values into its financial statements.
- **Tata Consultancy Services (TCS):** TCS employs the discounted cash flows method to estimate the long-term economic contributions of its workforce. This method helps the company understand the future cash flows generated by its human resources and make informed strategic decisions.

Conclusion

Income-based methods in Human Resource Accounting provide valuable insights into the future economic benefits generated by human resources. By applying these methods, organizations can quantify the value of their workforce based on projected future earnings, support strategic planning, and enhance decision-making. Despite challenges, the benefits of income-based methods make them a valuable tool for understanding and managing the economic contributions of human resources in a dynamic business environment.

CHAPTER TWELVE

Applications of Human Resource Accounting

Introduction to Applications of Human Resource Accounting

Human Resource Accounting (HRA) is a powerful tool that provides valuable insights into the value and contributions of an organization's workforce. By measuring and reporting the economic value of human resources, HRA supports various applications that enhance decision-making, strategic planning, and overall organizational performance. This chapter explores the key applications of HRA in different organizational contexts.

Key Applications of Human Resource Accounting

Strategic Human Resource Management (HRM)

Strategic Human Resource Management (HRM) involves aligning human resource practices with an organization's goals and strategic objectives to enhance overall performance and competitiveness. Human Resource Accounting (HRA) plays a crucial role in this process by providing data-driven insights that quantify the value of human resources. These insights help organizations make informed decisions about key HR functions such as recruitment, training, development, and retention. By understanding the economic value and potential contributions of their workforce, organizations can devise strategies that optimize employee performance and engagement. This alignment of HR practices with organizational goals not only supports the achievement of strategic objectives but also fosters a culture of continuous improvement and competitive advantage. Ultimately, strategic HRM ensures that human resources are effectively utilized to drive organizational success.

Performance Evaluation and Management

Performance Evaluation and Management is a vital aspect of any organization's success, and Human Resource Accounting (HRA) provides a robust framework for this purpose. By quantifying the economic value generated by human resources, organizations can effectively evaluate employee performance and contributions. This data-driven approach allows for a more objective assessment of the effectiveness of HR policies and practices. Using HRA data, organizations can set performance benchmarks that serve as standards for evaluating employee achievements. Additionally, it helps identify areas for improvement, enabling the implementation of targeted development programs aimed at enhancing employee skills and productivity. By leveraging HRA for performance evaluation and management, organizations can ensure that their workforce remains aligned with strategic goals, fostering a culture of continuous improvement and driving overall organizational performance.

Financial Reporting and Transparency

Incorporating Human Resource Accounting (HRA) data into financial statements significantly enhances transparency and offers a more holistic view of an organization's assets and liabilities. By including the value of human resources in financial reporting, organizations can provide stakeholders with a clearer understanding of the economic contributions made by their workforce. This comprehensive view helps in showcasing the true value of human capital, which is often one of the most critical assets of an organization. Enhanced transparency through HRA fosters trust and confidence among investors, regulators, and other stakeholders, as they can better assess the organization's overall performance and strategic position. Additionally, it supports informed decision-making by presenting a more accurate picture of the organization's financial health and potential for future growth.

Incentive Compensation and Reward Systems

Human Resource Accounting (HRA) plays a pivotal role in designing incentive compensation and reward systems that align employees' interests with the overall goals of the organization. By linking compensation directly to the economic value generated by employees, organizations can effectively motivate and retain top talent. This approach not only fosters a performance-driven culture but also ensures that reward systems are perceived as fair, transparent, and based on measurable contributions. Using HRA data, companies can create compensation packages that reflect the true value of employees' efforts, promoting a sense of equity and recognition. Furthermore, such data-driven reward systems can help identify high-performing individuals and teams, providing them with appropriate incentives to continue delivering exceptional results. Ultimately, leveraging HRA for incentive compensation leads to enhanced employee satisfaction, productivity, and loyalty, contributing to the organization's long-term success.

Talent Management and Succession Planning

Talent Management and Succession Planning are crucial components of an organization's long-term success, and Human Resource Accounting (HRA) provides valuable insights to support these processes. By analyzing HRA data, organizations can gain a deeper understanding of the skills, performance, and potential of their employees. This information enables them to identify high-potential individuals who can be groomed for future leadership roles. Succession planning ensures that there is a pipeline of capable talent ready to step into key positions as they become available, minimizing disruptions and maintaining continuity.

Additionally, HRA data helps organizations develop targeted training and development programs that address specific skill gaps and enhance employee capabilities. By aligning talent management strategies with organizational goals, companies can ensure that they have the right people in the right roles, driving efficiency, innovation, and growth. Effective talent management and succession planning foster a culture of continuous improvement, enhance employee engagement, and contribute to the organization's overall competitiveness and sustainability.

Workforce Planning and Optimization

Workforce planning and optimization are essential for aligning an organization's human resources with its strategic objectives. Human Resource Accounting (HRA) plays a pivotal role in this process by providing comprehensive data on the cost and value of human resources. By analyzing HRA data, organizations can gain insights into existing skills gaps, anticipate future workforce needs, and efficiently allocate resources. This proactive approach allows businesses to develop targeted recruitment and training strategies, ensuring that they have the right talent in place to achieve their goals. Additionally, workforce planning helps in optimizing labor costs, enhancing productivity, and maintaining a competitive edge in the market. By leveraging HRA for workforce planning and optimization, organizations can build a resilient and agile workforce capable of driving long-term success and growth.

Cost Management and Efficiency Improvement

Human Resource Accounting (HRA) is an invaluable tool for cost management and efficiency improvement within organizations. By providing detailed insights into the costs associated with various human resource practices, HRA allows organizations to pinpoint areas where cost reductions can be achieved. Through the analysis of HRA data, businesses can streamline their HR processes, reducing unnecessary expenditures and enhancing overall efficiency.

One key area where HRA proves beneficial is in identifying and addressing high turnover rates. By understanding the financial impact of turnover, organizations can implement strategies to improve employee retention, thereby saving on recruitment and training costs. Additionally, HRA data can be used to optimize investment in employee development programs, ensuring that resources are allocated effectively to enhance skills and productivity.

Furthermore, HRA helps in evaluating the cost-effectiveness of current HR policies and practices, providing a clear picture of their return on investment. By using this information, organizations can make informed decisions about where to allocate resources to achieve the best outcomes. Ultimately, leveraging HRA for cost management and efficiency improvement leads to a more financially sustainable and high-performing organization.

Compliance and Risk Management

Compliance and risk management are critical aspects of effective human resource management, and Human Resource Accounting (HRA) plays a vital role in supporting these functions. By providing accurate and transparent reporting of human resource data, HRA ensures that organizations comply with relevant regulations and standards related to HR management and accounting. This transparency helps mitigate legal and regulatory risks, providing a clear picture of HR-related practices and their financial implications.

Additionally, HRA aids in identifying and addressing potential HR-related risks such as workforce shortages, skill gaps, and compliance with labor laws. By analyzing HRA data, organizations can proactively manage these risks, implementing strategies to ensure that they have the necessary talent and skills to meet their strategic objectives. This proactive approach not only enhances compliance but also helps in maintaining a stable and capable workforce, ultimately contributing to the organization's long-term success and sustainability.

Case Studies and Examples

- **Infosys Limited:** Infosys uses HRA to support its strategic HRM and talent management initiatives. By quantifying the value of its human resources, Infosys can make informed decisions about recruitment, training, and development programs. HRA data also supports performance evaluation and incentive compensation systems, ensuring alignment with organizational goals.
- **Tata Consultancy Services (TCS):** TCS incorporates HRA data into its financial reporting to enhance transparency and provide stakeholders with a comprehensive view of its workforce's economic contributions. The company uses HRA to design incentive compensation systems that motivate and retain top talent. HRA data also supports workforce planning and optimization, helping TCS achieve its strategic objectives.

Conclusion

Human Resource Accounting has numerous applications that enhance decision-making, strategic planning, and overall organizational performance. By quantifying the value and contributions of human resources, HRA provides valuable insights that support various HR and financial practices. Despite challenges, the benefits of HRA make it a valuable tool for modern organizations committed to optimizing their workforce and achieving sustainable growth.

CHAPTER THIRTEEN

RECRUITMENT AND SELECTION

Introduction to Recruitment and Selection

Recruitment and selection are crucial components of Human Resource Management (HRM) and play a significant role in acquiring the right talent for an organization. Effective recruitment and selection processes ensure that organizations attract, identify, and hire individuals with the necessary skills, knowledge, and abilities to achieve their strategic goals. This chapter explores the key aspects of recruitment and selection, their importance, and best practices for optimizing these processes.

Recruitment: Attracting Talent

- **Defining Recruitment:** Recruitment is the process of identifying, attracting, and engaging potential candidates to fill job vacancies within an organization. It involves various activities, such as job posting, advertising, sourcing, and employer branding.
- **Recruitment Process:** Job Analysis and Job Description: Conducting a job analysis to understand the requirements of the position and creating a detailed job description that outlines the responsibilities, qualifications, and competencies needed for the role.
- **Sourcing Candidates:** Identifying potential candidates through various channels, such as job boards, social media, employee referrals, recruitment agencies, and career fairs.
- **Employer Branding:** Building and promoting a strong employer brand to attract top talent. This includes showcasing the organization's culture, values, benefits, and growth opportunities.

- **Advertising Job Vacancies:** Posting job openings on relevant platforms to reach a wide audience of potential candidates.
- **Applicant Tracking System (ATS):** Using an ATS to manage and streamline the recruitment process, track applications, and maintain candidate databases.
- **Selection:** Choosing the Right Candidate
- **Defining Selection:** Selection is the process of evaluating and choosing the most suitable candidate from a pool of applicants. It involves various assessment methods to determine the candidate's fit with the job requirements and organizational culture.

Selection Process:

- **Screening Applications:** Reviewing resumes and applications to shortlist candidates who meet the minimum qualifications and requirements.
- **Preliminary Interviews:** Conducting initial interviews to assess the candidate's suitability and gather additional information about their background and experience.
- **Assessment Methods:** Using various assessment methods, such as cognitive ability tests, personality assessments, work samples, and situational judgment tests, to evaluate the candidate's skills and competencies.
- **Behavioral Interviews:** Conducting behavioral interviews to assess the candidate's past experiences and how they align with the job requirements. Behavioral interviews focus on specific examples of how candidates have demonstrated relevant competencies in previous roles.
- **Reference Checks:** Contacting references provided by the candidate to verify their qualifications, work history, and performance.
- **Final Interviews:** Conducting final interviews with key decision-makers to make the final selection decision.
- **Job Offer and Negotiation:** Extending a job offer to the selected candidate and negotiating the terms of employment, such as salary, benefits, and start date.

Importance of Recruitment and Selection

- **Talent Acquisition:** Effective recruitment and selection processes enable organizations to attract and acquire top talent, ensuring that they have the right people in the right roles.

- **Organizational Performance:** The quality of an organization's workforce directly impacts its performance and success. By selecting the right candidates, organizations can enhance productivity, innovation, and overall effectiveness.
- **Employee Retention:** A well-designed recruitment and selection process helps ensure that new hires are a good fit for the organization, reducing turnover and increasing employee retention.
- **Cost Efficiency:** Efficient recruitment and selection processes minimize the costs associated with hiring, onboarding, and training new employees. Reducing turnover also lowers the costs of replacing employees.
- **Compliance and Diversity:** Recruitment and selection processes must comply with legal and regulatory requirements, such as equal employment opportunity laws. Additionally, promoting diversity and inclusion in hiring practices enhances the organization's culture and competitiveness.

Best Practices for Recruitment and Selection

- **Define Clear Job Requirements:** Conduct a thorough job analysis to identify the key responsibilities, qualifications, and competencies needed for the role. Create detailed job descriptions to attract the right candidates.
- **Leverage Technology:** Use technology, such as Applicant Tracking Systems (ATS) and recruitment software, to streamline the recruitment process, manage applications, and improve candidate experience.
- **Promote Employer Branding:** Build a strong employer brand to attract top talent. Showcase the organization's culture, values, and benefits through various channels, such as social media, company website, and employee testimonials.
- **Use Multiple Sourcing Channels:** Diversify sourcing channels to reach a wide pool of potential candidates. Consider job boards, social media, employee referrals, recruitment agencies, and career fairs.
- **Implement Structured Interviews:** Use structured interviews with standardized questions to ensure a fair and consistent evaluation of candidates. Behavioral interviews can provide valuable insights into the candidate's past performance and potential.

- **Conduct Thorough Assessments:** Use a combination of assessment methods, such as cognitive ability tests, personality assessments, and work samples, to evaluate the candidate's skills and competencies.
- **Ensure Compliance and Diversity:** Adhere to legal and regulatory requirements in the recruitment and selection process. Promote diversity and inclusion by implementing unbiased hiring practices and actively seeking diverse candidates.
- **Provide a Positive Candidate Experience:** Communicate regularly with candidates, provide timely feedback, and ensure a smooth and respectful hiring process. A positive candidate experience enhances the organization's reputation and attractiveness to top talent.

Conclusion

Recruitment and selection are critical processes that determine the quality of an organization's workforce. By implementing effective and efficient recruitment and selection practices, organizations can attract, identify, and hire the right talent, enhancing their performance and competitiveness. Despite challenges, the benefits of a well-designed recruitment and selection process make it a valuable tool for modern organizations committed to achieving sustainable growth and success.

CHAPTER FOURTEEN

Training and Development

Introduction to Training and Development

Training and development are vital components of Human Resource Management (HRM) that focus on enhancing employees' skills, knowledge, and abilities. Effective training and development programs help organizations achieve their strategic goals by ensuring that employees are well-equipped to perform their roles and adapt to changing business needs. This chapter explores the key aspects of training and development, their importance, and best practices for implementing successful programs.

Importance of Training and Development

- **Skill Enhancement:** Skill enhancement through training and development programs is essential for improving employee performance and productivity. These programs provide opportunities for employees to acquire new skills and refine existing ones, keeping them up-to-date with industry trends and technological advancements. By investing in continuous learning, organizations can foster a culture of growth and innovation, ensuring that their workforce remains competitive and capable of meeting evolving business demands. Furthermore, training and development initiatives contribute to higher employee morale and job satisfaction, as employees feel valued and empowered to reach their full potential. Ultimately, a well-trained and skilled workforce drives organizational success and helps maintain a sustainable competitive advantage.

- **Employee Engagement and Retention:** Fostering employee engagement and retention is critical for organizational success. By providing opportunities for learning and growth, organizations can significantly enhance employee satisfaction and engagement. When employees feel valued and see a clear path for career advancement, they are more likely to be motivated and committed to their roles. This sense of fulfillment translates into increased loyalty and a stronger connection to the organization.

Investing in training and development programs not only equips employees with the necessary skills to perform their jobs effectively but also demonstrates the organization's commitment to their professional growth. This approach reduces turnover rates by retaining top talent who might otherwise seek opportunities elsewhere. Furthermore, engaged employees are more productive, contribute to a positive work environment, and are more likely to advocate for the organization. Overall, a focus on employee engagement and retention through continuous learning and growth opportunities drives long-term success and creates a thriving organizational culture.

- **Organizational Performance:** A skilled and knowledgeable workforce is a cornerstone of organizational performance. Employees equipped with up-to-date skills and knowledge can drive innovation by developing new ideas, processes, and products. Their expertise enables them to tackle complex challenges efficiently, leading to higher productivity and operational excellence. Additionally, a capable workforce enhances an organization's competitiveness in the market by delivering superior quality and value to customers. By continuously investing in employee development, organizations can ensure sustained growth and adaptability, ultimately leading to long-term success and a stronger market position.

- **Adaptability to Change:** Adaptability to change is a crucial factor in maintaining an organization's agility and responsiveness to evolving market demands, new technologies, and innovative processes. Training and development programs play a significant role in fostering this adaptability among employees. By equipping them with the necessary skills and knowledge, organizations ensure their workforce is prepared to embrace and implement changes effectively. Continuous learning initiatives help employees stay current with industry advancements, reduce resistance to change, and enhance their ability to navigate and thrive in dynamic environments. As a result, organizations that prioritize adaptability through comprehensive training and development can maintain a competitive edge, quickly respond to market shifts, and drive sustained growth and innovation.

- **Compliance and Safety:** Compliance and safety are critical elements in any organization, and effective training programs play a vital role in maintaining both. By educating employees on legal and regulatory requirements, these programs ensure that staff members are well-informed about the standards and protocols they must follow. This knowledge helps prevent legal issues and promotes adherence to industry regulations. Additionally, training programs emphasize the importance of workplace safety, teaching employees how to identify and mitigate potential hazards. This proactive approach not only protects employees from harm but also fosters a culture of safety and responsibility. Ultimately, well-designed training programs contribute to a compliant and safe work environment, enhancing overall organizational performance and reducing the risk of accidents and legal complications.

Types of Training and Development Programs

Onboarding and Orientation

Onboarding programs introduce new employees to the organization, its culture, policies, and procedures. Orientation sessions provide essential information to help new hires acclimate to their roles and integrate into the team.

Technical and Job-Specific Training

Technical training focuses on developing employees' job-specific skills and knowledge. It includes training on software, equipment, processes, and industry-specific practices. This type of training ensures employees can perform their tasks effectively and efficiently.

Soft Skills Training

Soft skills training focuses on developing interpersonal and communication skills, such as leadership, teamwork, conflict resolution, and emotional intelligence. These skills are critical for building strong relationships, enhancing collaboration, and fostering a positive work environment.

Leadership and Management Development

Leadership and management development programs aim to build the capabilities of current and future leaders. These programs include training on strategic thinking, decision-making, team management, and other leadership competencies. Developing strong leaders is essential for driving organizational success and achieving long-term goals.

Compliance and Safety Training

Compliance training ensures that employees understand and adhere to legal and regulatory requirements, such as workplace safety, anti-discrimination laws, and data protection regulations. Safety training focuses on promoting safe work practices and preventing accidents and injuries.

Professional Development and Continuing Education

Professional development programs support employees' ongoing learning and growth. These programs include workshops, seminars, conferences, certification courses, and advanced degree programs. Encouraging continuous learning helps employees stay current with industry trends and best practices.

Steps in Implementing Training and Development Programs

- **Needs Assessment:** Conduct a needs assessment to identify the skills gaps and training requirements of employees. This involves analyzing job roles, performance data, and feedback from managers and employees.
- **Program Design:** Develop a training program that addresses the identified needs. Design the content, format, and delivery methods to ensure the program is engaging, relevant, and effective.
- **Resource Allocation:** Allocate the necessary resources, including budget, training materials, and qualified trainers, to support the implementation of the training program.
- **Delivery and Implementation:** Deliver the training program using various methods, such as classroom training, e-learning, on-the-job training, and workshops. Ensure that the training is accessible and convenient for employees.
- **Evaluation and Feedback:** Evaluate the effectiveness of the training program by collecting feedback from participants and measuring improvements in performance. Use the feedback to make necessary adjustments and continuously improve the program.
- **Follow-Up and Support:** Provide ongoing support and follow-up to reinforce the learning and ensure employees can apply the new skills and knowledge in their roles. Offer additional training and development opportunities as needed.

Best Practices for Training and Development

- **Align with Organizational Goals:** Ensure that training and development programs are aligned with the organization's strategic objectives and goals. This alignment ensures that the programs contribute to the overall success of the organization.
- **Use a Variety of Training Methods:** Employ a mix of training methods, such as classroom training, e-learning, on-the-job training, and coaching, to cater to different learning styles and preferences.
- **Encourage Continuous Learning:** Promote a culture of continuous learning by providing ongoing development opportunities and encouraging employees to take ownership of their learning and growth.
- **Measure and Evaluate:** Regularly measure the effectiveness of training programs through assessments, feedback, and performance metrics. Use the data to make informed decisions and improve the programs.
- **Engage and Empower Employees:** Involve employees in the design and implementation of training programs to ensure they are relevant and engaging. Empower employees to take an active role in their development.
- **Leverage Technology:** Use technology, such as learning management systems (LMS), virtual classrooms, and online resources, to deliver training programs efficiently and effectively.

Case Studies and Examples

- **Infosys Limited:** Infosys has a comprehensive training and development program that includes onboarding, technical training, leadership development, and continuous learning opportunities. The Infosys Global Education Center in Mysore, India, provides extensive training to new hires and ongoing development to existing employees, ensuring they are well-equipped to meet the organization's needs.
- **Tata Consultancy Services (TCS):** TCS invests in employee development through its various training programs, including technical training, soft skills development, and leadership training. The company's emphasis on continuous learning and development has contributed to its success and growth in the IT industry.

Conclusion

Training and development are essential for building a skilled, knowledgeable, and adaptable workforce. By implementing effective training and development programs, organizations can enhance employee performance, engagement, and retention, driving overall organizational success. Despite challenges, the benefits of a well-designed training and development strategy make it a valuable tool for modern organizations committed to achieving sustainable growth and excellence.

CHAPTER FIFTEEN

PERFORMANCE EVALUATION

Introduction to Performance Evaluation

Performance evaluation, also known as performance appraisal or performance review, is a critical process in Human Resource Management (HRM) that involves assessing employees' job performance and contributions to the organization. Effective performance evaluation provides valuable insights into employees' strengths and areas for improvement, supports career development, and informs decision-making related to promotions, rewards, and training. This chapter explores the key aspects of performance evaluation, its importance, and best practices for conducting meaningful evaluations.

Importance of Performance Evaluation

- **Employee Development:** Employee development is a key aspect of organizational growth, and performance evaluations play a crucial role in this process. By conducting regular performance assessments, organizations can identify areas where employees excel and pinpoint areas that require improvement. The insights gained from these evaluations are then used to create personalized development plans tailored to each employee's unique needs and goals. These plans may include targeted training programs, mentorship opportunities, and skill-building initiatives designed to enhance employees' competencies and support their professional growth. By investing in personalized development, organizations can ensure that their workforce remains skilled, motivated, and capable of driving the company's success. Moreover, it fosters a culture of continuous improvement, where employees feel valued and empowered to reach their full potential.

- **Goal Alignment:** Goal alignment is essential for achieving organizational success, and performance evaluations play a crucial role in this process. By conducting regular evaluations, organizations can assess individual employee goals and performance, ensuring they are in line with broader organizational objectives. This alignment helps to create a unified direction, where all employees understand and work towards common strategic goals. It fosters a sense of purpose and accountability, as employees can clearly see how their contributions impact the overall success of the organization. Additionally, aligning goals facilitates better communication and collaboration, as teams are aware of each other's priorities and can work together more effectively. Overall, goal alignment through performance evaluations ensures that everyone is moving in the same direction, maximizing efficiency and driving organizational growth.

- **Motivation and Engagement:** Motivation and engagement are vital components of a thriving workplace, and regular feedback along with recognition of achievements play a significant role in fostering these qualities. By providing consistent and constructive feedback, organizations help employees understand their strengths and areas for improvement, guiding them toward better performance and growth. Recognition of achievements, whether through formal awards or simple acknowledgments, reinforces positive behavior and makes employees feel valued for their contributions. This recognition boosts morale and motivates employees to maintain high levels of performance. A positive work environment, where employees feel appreciated and supported, enhances overall engagement, leading to increased productivity, job satisfaction, and organizational loyalty. Ultimately, regular feedback and recognition create a culture of appreciation and continuous improvement, driving the organization towards sustained success.

- **Informed Decision-Making:** Informed decision-making is a cornerstone of effective human resource management, and performance evaluations provide critical data to support this process. By systematically assessing employee performance, organizations gather valuable insights into individual achievements, strengths, and areas for improvement. This data is instrumental in making decisions about promotions, ensuring that high-performing employees are recognized and advanced within the organization.

Additionally, performance evaluations inform salary adjustments by providing a basis for rewarding exceptional performance and addressing discrepancies in compensation. This approach ensures fairness and motivates employees to strive for excellence.

Identifying training needs is another key benefit of performance evaluations. By pinpointing skill gaps and areas where employees could benefit from additional development, organizations can design targeted training programs to enhance overall workforce capabilities.

Finally, performance evaluations play a crucial role in succession planning. By understanding the potential of employees and their readiness for leadership roles, organizations can strategically plan for future talent needs, ensuring continuity and stability in key positions.

Overall, the data derived from performance evaluations enables organizations to make well-informed, strategic decisions that enhance employee development, satisfaction, and organizational performance.

- **Accountability:** Accountability is a fundamental aspect of performance evaluations, which hold employees responsible for their actions and results. By setting clear expectations and regularly assessing performance, evaluations create a sense of ownership among employees regarding their responsibilities and outcomes. This accountability fosters a culture of transparency and integrity, where employees are aware of their roles and the impact of their work on the organization's success. It encourages them to actively engage in their tasks, strive for excellence, and take initiative to improve their performance. Additionally, accountability through performance evaluations helps identify areas needing support or development, ensuring that employees receive the necessary resources to succeed. Ultimately, this process promotes a high-performance culture where individuals are motivated to contribute their best, driving overall organizational growth and efficiency.

- **Compliance and Legal Protection:** Documenting performance evaluations is a crucial practice for compliance and legal protection within an organization. By maintaining accurate and detailed records of employee performance, organizations create a reliable account of each individual's work history, achievements, and areas needing improvement. This documentation serves as evidence to support employment decisions such as promotions, terminations, and disciplinary actions, ensuring they are based on objective and consistent criteria.

In legal matters, having well-documented performance evaluations can be invaluable. They provide a factual basis for defending against claims of wrongful termination, discrimination, or other employment-related disputes. Comprehensive records demonstrate that the organization follows fair and transparent evaluation processes, reinforcing its commitment to equitable treatment of employees. Additionally, these documents help ensure compliance with labor laws and regulations, reducing the risk of legal challenges and potential penalties.

Overall, maintaining thorough documentation of performance evaluations enhances the organization's ability to make informed, fair, and legally sound employment decisions, while also fostering a culture of accountability and transparency.

Key Components of Performance Evaluation

- **Setting Performance Standards:** Establish clear and measurable performance standards based on job descriptions and organizational goals. These standards serve as benchmarks for evaluating employee performance.
- **Goal Setting:** Collaboratively set individual performance goals with employees, ensuring that they align with organizational objectives. Goals should be Specific, Measurable, Achievable, Relevant, and Time-bound (SMART).
- **Ongoing Feedback:** Provide continuous feedback throughout the evaluation period, rather than waiting for the formal review. Regular feedback helps employees understand their progress and make necessary adjustments.
- **Self-Assessment:** Encourage employees to conduct self-assessments, reflecting on their achievements, challenges, and areas for improvement. Self-assessment promotes self-awareness and ownership of performance.
- **360-Degree Feedback:** Gather feedback from multiple sources, including peers, subordinates, and supervisors, to provide a comprehensive view of an employee's performance. 360-degree feedback helps identify strengths and development areas from different perspectives.

- **Performance Metrics:** Use objective performance metrics to evaluate employees. These metrics may include key performance indicators (KPIs), productivity measures, quality of work, and achievement of goals.
- **Performance Review Meeting:** Conduct formal performance review meetings to discuss the evaluation results, provide feedback, and set future goals. These meetings should be constructive, focusing on both achievements and development opportunities.
- **Development Plans:** Create individualized development plans based on the evaluation results. These plans outline specific actions, training, and support needed to help employees improve their performance and achieve their career goals.

Best Practices for Performance Evaluation

- **Be Objective and Fair:** Ensure that performance evaluations are objective, unbiased, and based on factual evidence. Avoid personal biases and ensure consistency in the evaluation process.
- **Provide Specific Feedback:** Offer specific examples and evidence to support feedback. Avoid vague or general statements, and focus on actionable insights.
- **Foster Open Communication:** Create an environment where employees feel comfortable sharing their thoughts, concerns, and aspirations during the evaluation process. Encourage open dialogue and active listening.
- **Focus on Development:** Emphasize development and growth rather than solely focusing on past performance. Identify opportunities for training, coaching, and skill enhancement.
- **Regularly Review and Update Goals:** Continuously review and update performance goals to ensure they remain relevant and aligned with organizational objectives. Adjust goals as needed to reflect changing priorities and circumstances.
- **Recognize and Reward Achievements:** Acknowledge and reward employees' accomplishments and contributions. Recognition can be in the form of verbal praise, bonuses, promotions, or other incentives.
- **Document the Evaluation:** Maintain thorough documentation of performance evaluations, including feedback, goals, and development plans. This documentation provides a valuable record for future reference.

Challenges in Performance Evaluation

- **Subjectivity and Bias:** Performance evaluations can be influenced by personal biases and subjective judgments, affecting the accuracy and fairness of the assessments.
- **Inconsistent Standards:** Variations in performance standards and evaluation criteria across different departments or managers can lead to inconsistencies in the evaluation process.
- **Lack of Timely Feedback:** Delayed or infrequent feedback reduces the effectiveness of performance evaluations and limits employees' ability to improve.
- **Resistance to Feedback:** Employees may be resistant to receiving feedback, especially if it is perceived as negative or critical. Effective communication and a supportive approach are essential to address this challenge.

Case Studies and Examples

- **Infosys Limited:** Infosys uses a comprehensive performance evaluation system that includes goal setting, ongoing feedback, self-assessment, and 360-degree feedback. The company's focus on continuous development and open communication has contributed to high employee engagement and performance.
- **Tata Consultancy Services (TCS):** TCS implements a structured performance evaluation process with clear performance metrics, regular feedback, and individualized development plans. The company's emphasis on recognizing and rewarding achievements has fostered a culture of excellence and innovation.

Conclusion

Performance evaluation is a critical process for assessing and improving employees' job performance and contributions to the organization. By implementing effective performance evaluation practices, organizations can enhance employee development, motivation, and engagement, leading to improved organizational performance. Despite challenges, the benefits of a well-designed performance evaluation system make it a valuable tool for modern organizations committed to achieving excellence and sustainable growth.

CHAPTER SIXTEEN

COMPENSATION AND BENEFITS

Introduction to Compensation and Benefits

Compensation and benefits are critical components of Human Resource Management (HRM) that play a significant role in attracting, motivating, and retaining employees. A well-designed compensation and benefits strategy ensures that employees are fairly rewarded for their contributions, enhances job satisfaction, and supports overall organizational performance. This chapter explores the key aspects of compensation and benefits, their importance, and best practices for developing and implementing effective compensation and benefits programs.

Importance of Compensation and Benefits

- **Attracting Talent:** Competitive compensation and benefits packages are essential for attracting top talent to the organization. Job seekers often consider these factors when evaluating job opportunities.
- **Employee Motivation and Retention:** Fair and competitive compensation and benefits motivate employees to perform at their best and increase their loyalty to the organization, reducing turnover.
- **Job Satisfaction:** Adequate compensation and benefits contribute to employees' overall job satisfaction and well-being, fostering a positive work environment.
- **Performance and Productivity:** Properly structured compensation and benefits packages align employees' interests with organizational goals, encouraging higher performance and productivity.
- **Legal Compliance:** Ensuring that compensation and benefits practices comply with legal and regulatory requirements helps organizations avoid

legal issues and maintain a positive reputation.

Components of Compensation

- **Base Salary:** The fixed amount of money paid to an employee for their job performance, usually expressed as an annual salary or hourly wage. Base salary is determined by factors such as job responsibilities, experience, education, and market benchmarks.
- **Incentive Pay:** Additional compensation based on achieving specific performance goals or targets. Incentive pay can include bonuses, commissions, and profit-sharing. It is designed to motivate employees to achieve higher performance levels.
- **Overtime Pay:** Compensation for hours worked beyond the standard workweek, typically paid at a higher rate. Overtime pay is often required by labor laws and regulations.
- **Allowances:** Additional payments to cover specific expenses related to the job, such as travel, housing, and transportation allowances. Allowances provide financial support for work-related expenses.
- **Equity Compensation:** Non-cash compensation that provides employees with ownership stakes in the company, such as stock options, restricted stock units (RSUs), and employee stock purchase plans (ESPPs). Equity compensation aligns employees' interests with the long-term success of the organization.

Components of Benefits

- **Health and Wellness Benefits:** Benefits that support employees' physical and mental health, including health insurance, dental and vision coverage, wellness programs, and employee assistance programs (EAPs).
- **Retirement Benefits:** Financial plans that help employees save for retirement, such as pension plans, 401(k) plans, and employer contributions to retirement accounts.
- **Paid Time Off (PTO):** Benefits that provide employees with paid leave for vacation, holidays, sick days, and personal days. PTO policies vary by organization and may include additional leave for specific purposes, such as parental leave.
- **Flexible Work Arrangements:** Benefits that offer flexibility in work schedules and locations, such as remote work options, flexible hours, and

compressed workweeks. These arrangements support work-life balance and employee well-being.

- **Education and Professional Development:** Benefits that support employees' ongoing learning and career growth, including tuition reimbursement, training programs, and professional development opportunities.
- **Other Perks and Benefits:** Additional benefits that enhance employees' overall experience, such as employee discounts, wellness programs, childcare support, and transportation subsidies.

Best Practices for Compensation and Benefits Programs

- **Conduct Market Research:** Regularly conduct market research to understand industry compensation and benefits trends and benchmarks. This ensures that the organization's offerings are competitive and attractive to potential and current employees.
- **Align with Organizational Goals:** Ensure that compensation and benefits programs align with the organization's strategic objectives and goals. This alignment helps motivate employees to contribute to the organization's success.
- **Maintain Fairness and Transparency:** Establish clear and consistent policies for compensation and benefits, ensuring fairness and transparency in their administration. Communicate these policies effectively to employees.
- **Offer a Mix of Compensation and Benefits:** Provide a balanced mix of monetary and non-monetary compensation, as well as comprehensive benefits that address employees' diverse needs and preferences.
- **Regularly Review and Adjust:** Regularly review and adjust compensation and benefits programs to reflect changes in the market, organizational goals, and employee needs. This ensures that the programs remain relevant and competitive.
- **Promote Employee Participation:** Involve employees in the design and evaluation of compensation and benefits programs. Seek feedback to understand their preferences and ensure that the programs meet their needs.
- **Focus on Total Rewards:** Adopt a total rewards approach that considers all aspects of compensation, benefits, recognition, and development opportunities. This holistic view ensures that employees feel valued and

rewarded in multiple ways.

Challenges in Compensation and Benefits

- **Budget Constraints:** Limited financial resources can restrict the organization's ability to offer competitive compensation and benefits packages.
- **Regulatory Compliance:** Navigating complex labor laws and regulations related to compensation and benefits can be challenging. Non-compliance can result in legal issues and penalties.
- **Market Fluctuations:** Changes in the labor market and economic conditions can impact compensation and benefits trends, requiring organizations to adapt their programs accordingly.
- **Diverse Workforce Needs:** Employees have diverse needs and preferences, making it challenging to design compensation and benefits programs that cater to everyone.

Case Studies and Examples

- **Infosys Limited:** Infosys offers a comprehensive compensation and benefits program that includes competitive base salaries, performance-based incentives, health and wellness benefits, and professional development opportunities. The company's focus on total rewards has contributed to high employee satisfaction and retention.
- **Tata Consultancy Services (TCS):** TCS provides a range of benefits, including health insurance, retirement plans, paid time off, and flexible work arrangements. The company's commitment to employee well-being and work-life balance has enhanced its reputation as an employer of choice.

Conclusion

Compensation and benefits are essential for attracting, motivating, and retaining employees. By designing and implementing effective compensation and benefits programs, organizations can enhance job satisfaction, performance, and overall organizational success. Despite challenges, the benefits of a well-structured compensation and benefits strategy make it a valuable tool for modern organizations committed to achieving excellence and sustainable growth.

CHAPTER SEVENTEEN

CHALLENGES AND LIMITATIONS

Introduction to Challenges and Limitations

Human Resource Accounting (HRA) provides valuable insights into the value and contributions of an organization's workforce. However, like any management practice, HRA faces various challenges and limitations that can impact its effectiveness and implementation. This chapter explores the key challenges and limitations of HRA, along with strategies to address them.

Challenges in Human Resource Accounting
Data Availability and Accuracy

- **Challenge:** Accurate and comprehensive data on employee performance, skills, and potential can be difficult to obtain and measure. Incomplete or inaccurate data can lead to flawed HRA analyses and decisions.
- **Solution:** Implement robust data collection and management systems to ensure accurate and timely data. Regularly review and update data sources to maintain data integrity.

Subjectivity and Bias

- **Challenge:** Valuing human resources involves subjective estimates and judgments, which can introduce biases and inconsistencies in measurement and reporting.
- **Solution:** Use standardized and objective methods for HRA to minimize subjectivity. Incorporate multiple perspectives, such as 360-degree feedback, to obtain a comprehensive view of employee performance.

Lack of Standardization

- **Challenge:** The lack of standardized methods and practices for HRA can result in variations in how organizations measure and report human capital. This can make it challenging to compare HRA data across organizations.
- **Solution:** Advocate for industry standards and guidelines for HRA practices. Participate in professional associations and initiatives that promote standardized HRA methodologies.

Cost and Complexity

- **Challenge:** Implementing HRA can be expensive and time-consuming, requiring significant investment in data collection, analysis, and reporting. Smaller organizations may find it challenging to allocate resources for HRA.
- **Solution:** Prioritize key HRA initiatives that align with organizational goals and provide the most value. Consider leveraging technology and outsourcing certain HRA functions to reduce costs and complexity.

Employee Privacy and Confidentiality

- **Challenge:** Collecting and analyzing employee data for HRA purposes raises concerns about privacy and confidentiality. Inappropriate handling of sensitive data can lead to legal and ethical issues.
- **Solution:** Establish clear policies and procedures for data privacy and confidentiality. Ensure compliance with data protection regulations and obtain informed consent from employees for data collection.

Limitations of Human Resource Accounting
Intangible Nature of Human Resources

- **Limitation:** Human resources possess intangible qualities, such as creativity, leadership, and teamwork, that are difficult to quantify and value accurately. This makes it challenging to capture the full economic value of human capital.
- **Solution:** Use a combination of quantitative and qualitative methods to assess the value of intangible qualities. Incorporate metrics that reflect

the impact of these qualities on organizational performance.

Dynamic and Evolving Workforce

- **Limitation:** The workforce is dynamic and constantly evolving, with changing skills, roles, and expectations. HRA methods may struggle to keep pace with these changes and accurately reflect the current state of the workforce.
- **Solution:** Continuously update HRA practices to reflect changes in the workforce and market conditions. Implement regular reviews and adjustments to HRA methodologies.

Integration with Financial Reporting

- **Limitation:** Integrating HRA data into traditional financial reporting systems can be challenging. Financial statements primarily focus on tangible assets, and incorporating human capital values requires new accounting frameworks.
- **Solution:** Develop integrated reporting systems that combine financial and non-financial data. Collaborate with accounting professionals to create frameworks that accommodate HRA data.

Limited Predictive Power

- **Limitation:** HRA provides valuable historical and current insights into human resources but may have limited predictive power for future performance. Predicting future outcomes based on past data involves uncertainties and risks.
- **Solution:** Use HRA data in conjunction with predictive analytics and scenario planning to enhance future decision-making. Incorporate a range of factors and variables to improve the accuracy of predictions.

Resistance to Change

- **Limitation:** Organizations and employees may resist adopting HRA practices due to a lack of understanding, fear of change, or concerns about the implications of being evaluated.

- **Solution:** Promote awareness and understanding of HRA benefits through training and communication. Involve employees in the development and implementation of HRA practices to gain their support and buy-in.

Conclusion

Human Resource Accounting provides valuable insights into the value and contributions of an organization's workforce, but it also faces several challenges and limitations. By addressing these challenges and continuously improving HRA practices, organizations can enhance their ability to measure, manage, and report the value of human capital. Despite limitations, the benefits of HRA make it a valuable tool for modern organizations committed to optimizing their workforce and achieving sustainable growth.

CHAPTER EIGHTEEN

MEASUREMENT DIFFICULTIES

Introduction to Measurement Difficulties

Human Resource Accounting (HRA) involves quantifying the value of an organization's human resources, but this process is not without its challenges. Measuring the value of human resources accurately and consistently poses several difficulties that can impact the reliability and effectiveness of HRA. This chapter explores the key measurement difficulties in HRA and strategies to address them.

Key Measurement Difficulties

Intangibility of Human Resources

- **Difficulty:** Human resources possess intangible qualities like creativity, leadership, and teamwork, which are critical to organizational success but challenging to quantify and value accurately. Traditional accounting methods often fall short in capturing these qualities' true value, as they primarily focus on tangible assets and financial metrics. Creativity, for instance, drives innovation and problem-solving but is not easily measured in numerical terms. Leadership influences team dynamics and organizational culture, yet its impact can vary widely and is difficult to express in standard financial reports. Similarly, teamwork enhances collaboration and productivity, but its benefits are often reflected in less tangible outcomes such as employee satisfaction and morale. As a result, organizations need to adopt more holistic and qualitative approaches to evaluate and appreciate these intangible qualities, recognizing their essential role in achieving long-term success.

- **Strategy:** To effectively assess the value of intangible qualities, it's crucial to use a combination of quantitative and qualitative methods. This approach ensures a comprehensive evaluation that captures both measurable data and nuanced insights. Incorporate metrics that reflect the impact of these qualities on organizational performance, such as innovation rates, team collaboration scores, and leadership effectiveness. Quantitative methods like key performance indicators (KPIs) and leadership assessments provide numerical data, while qualitative methods such as interviews, focus groups, and observations offer deeper context and personal perspectives. By integrating both approaches, organizations can accurately evaluate intangible qualities and their contribution to success, allowing for targeted strategies to enhance creativity, leadership, and teamwork.

Subjectivity and Bias

- **Difficulty:** Valuing human resources is inherently complex, as it involves subjective estimates and judgments. This subjectivity can introduce biases and inconsistencies in how human resource value is measured and reported. Different evaluators may have varying perspectives on the worth of qualities like creativity, leadership, and teamwork, leading to discrepancies in assessments. Moreover, these intangible qualities are not easily quantifiable using traditional accounting methods, which primarily focus on tangible assets. As a result, organizations may face challenges in achieving a consistent and objective evaluation of their human resources, making it difficult to accurately reflect their true value in financial and performance reports.
- **Strategy:** To minimize subjectivity in Human Resource Analytics (HRA), it is essential to use standardized and objective methods. This ensures consistent and unbiased evaluation of employee performance. Additionally, implementing multiple perspectives, such as 360-degree feedback, can provide a comprehensive view of an employee's performance by incorporating input from peers, supervisors, subordinates, and even the employees themselves. This holistic approach helps reduce biases and offers a more balanced assessment, leading to fairer and more accurate evaluations. By combining standardized methods with diverse perspectives, organizations can enhance the objectivity and reliability of their HRA practices.

Data Availability and Accuracy

- **Difficulty:** Accurate and comprehensive data on employee performance, skills, and potential can be challenging to obtain and measure. Incomplete or inaccurate data can lead to flawed HRA analyses and decisions.
- **Strategy:** Implement robust data collection and management systems to ensure accurate and timely data. Regularly review and update data sources to maintain data integrity. Use technology, such as HR analytics tools, to enhance data accuracy and accessibility.

Dynamic and Evolving Workforce

- **Difficulty:** The workforce is indeed dynamic, continually evolving with new skills, roles, and expectations. This constant change presents a significant challenge for Human Resource Analytics (HRA) methods, which may struggle to keep pace and accurately reflect the current state of the workforce. As employees acquire new skills and adapt to shifting roles, traditional HRA methods may become outdated or fail to capture the full range of competencies and contributions. Additionally, evolving expectations from employees regarding work-life balance, remote work, and career development require HRA to be more adaptive and responsive. This fluid environment demands that HRA practices are continually updated and refined to ensure they provide relevant and timely insights, accurately reflecting the workforce's current composition and needs. Without this agility, HRA may fall short in supporting strategic HR decisions and fostering organizational growth.
- **Strategy:** To ensure Human Resource Analytics (HRA) practices remain relevant and accurate, it is crucial to continuously update them in response to changes in the workforce and market conditions. This dynamic approach involves regularly reviewing and adjusting HRA methodologies to reflect the evolving skills, roles, and expectations of employees. By staying attuned to shifts in the labor market, technological advancements, and industry trends, organizations can adapt their HRA practices to better capture the current state of the workforce.

  Implementing regular reviews and updates helps identify areas where existing methodologies may be falling short or becoming outdated. This proactive stance allows organizations to refine their data collection and analysis processes, ensuring they provide meaningful and timely insights. Additionally, involving HR professionals, managers, and employees in the review process can offer valuable perspectives and feedback, further enhancing the accuracy and effectiveness of HRA practices.

By maintaining a flexible and adaptive approach to HRA, organizations can better support strategic HR decisions, enhance employee development, and drive organizational growth. This commitment to continuous improvement ensures that HRA remains a powerful tool for understanding and leveraging the full potential of the workforce.

Integration with Financial Reporting

- **Difficulty:** Integrating Human Resource Analytics (HRA) data into traditional financial reporting systems presents a significant challenge because financial statements are designed to focus on tangible assets, such as property, equipment, and inventory. These statements do not typically account for the intangible value of human capital, which includes the skills, knowledge, and capabilities of employees.

  To incorporate human capital values, organizations need to develop new accounting frameworks that recognize and quantify these intangible assets. This involves creating methodologies to measure the economic impact of employee attributes like creativity, leadership, and teamwork. However, developing these frameworks can be complex and requires careful consideration to ensure accuracy and consistency.

  Additionally, integrating HRA data with financial reporting necessitates cross-functional collaboration between HR and finance teams. They must work together to align their data collection, analysis, and reporting processes, ensuring that HRA insights are effectively translated into financial metrics. This integration also requires investment in technology and systems that can seamlessly manage and analyze both HR and financial data.

  Ultimately, incorporating human capital values into financial reporting can provide a more comprehensive view of an organization's true worth, highlighting the critical role of employees in driving business success. However, achieving this integration demands innovative accounting practices, robust methodologies, and collaborative efforts across the organization.

- **Strategy:** To effectively integrate Human Resource Analytics (HRA) data with traditional financial reporting, it's essential to develop integrated reporting systems that combine both financial and non-financial data. This approach provides a comprehensive view of organizational performance by highlighting the value of intangible assets such as employee skills, creativity, and leadership alongside tangible assets.

Collaboration with accounting professionals is crucial for creating frameworks that accommodate HRA data. These frameworks should be designed to measure and quantify the impact of human capital on financial outcomes, ensuring that HRA insights are consistently and accurately reflected in financial reports. Accounting professionals can offer valuable expertise in aligning HRA methodologies with established accounting principles, helping to create robust and reliable metrics.

Implementing integrated reporting systems also requires investment in technology and tools that can seamlessly manage and analyze both financial and non-financial data. Advanced analytics platforms and data management systems can support this integration by providing real-time insights and facilitating data-driven decision-making.

By developing integrated reporting systems and collaborating with accounting professionals, organizations can better capture the true value of their human resources and make more informed strategic decisions. This holistic approach not only enhances transparency and accountability but also underscores the critical role of human capital in driving organizational success.

Cost and Complexity

- **Difficulty:** Implementing Human Resource Analytics (HRA) can indeed be both expensive and time-consuming, posing significant challenges for organizations. The process requires substantial investment in various aspects, including data collection, analysis, and reporting. Acquiring advanced analytics tools and technologies, training staff, and maintaining data security protocols all contribute to the overall cost. Moreover, the time required to establish and refine HRA practices can strain organizational resources, particularly in smaller organizations with limited budgets.

Smaller organizations may find it difficult to allocate the necessary resources for comprehensive HRA initiatives. They might lack the financial capacity to invest in sophisticated analytics platforms or hire specialized personnel to manage and interpret HR data. Additionally, the time and effort required to implement HRA effectively could divert attention from other critical business operations.

To address these challenges, smaller organizations can explore cost-effective alternatives, such as leveraging existing tools and technologies, partnering with external consultants, or adopting a phased approach to HRA implementation. By prioritizing key areas and gradually expanding their HRA capabilities, smaller organizations can still benefit from data-driven insights without overwhelming their resources.

- **Strategy:** To effectively implement Human Resource Analytics (HRA) without overwhelming resources, it is crucial to prioritize key HRA initiatives that align with organizational goals and offer the most value. Begin by identifying the specific areas where HRA can have the most significant impact, such as improving employee performance, enhancing talent acquisition, or increasing employee engagement. Focusing on these priority areas ensures that efforts are concentrated on initiatives that directly contribute to achieving strategic objectives.

Leveraging technology can help reduce costs and complexity associated with HRA. Utilizing existing tools and software that offer analytics capabilities can streamline data collection, analysis, and reporting processes. Many affordable HRA solutions are available that provide robust features tailored to small and medium-sized enterprises.

Outsourcing certain HRA functions can also be a cost-effective strategy. Partnering with external consultants or specialized firms allows organizations to access expertise and advanced analytics without the need for significant internal investments. Outsourcing can be particularly beneficial for tasks such as data analysis, report generation, and compliance monitoring, where external providers can offer specialized skills and resources.

By prioritizing key initiatives, leveraging technology, and considering outsourcing options, organizations can implement HRA in a manageable and cost-effective manner, ultimately driving better decision-making and organizational performance.

Resistance to Change

- **Difficulty:** Organizations and employees may resist adopting Human Resource Analytics (HRA) practices for several reasons, primarily due to a lack of understanding, fear of change, or concerns about being evaluated. A lack of understanding about HRA's benefits and processes can lead to skepticism and resistance. Employees and managers might not fully grasp how HRA can improve decision-making, enhance employee development, and contribute to overall organizational success.

  Fear of change is another significant barrier. Implementing HRA often requires shifts in organizational culture, processes, and practices, which can be daunting. Employees may worry about how these changes will impact their roles, workloads, and job security. Additionally, concerns about being evaluated through HRA can create anxiety. Employees might fear that their data will be used unfairly or that the analytics will highlight their weaknesses, leading to negative consequences.

  To address these challenges, organizations must invest in education and communication. Providing clear, transparent information about HRA's purpose, benefits, and processes can help demystify the practice and build buy-in. Offering training and support can ease the transition and reassure employees that HRA is a tool for growth and improvement rather than a punitive measure. By addressing these concerns thoughtfully, organizations can foster a more receptive environment for adopting HRA practices.

- **Strategy:** Promoting awareness and understanding of Human Resource Analytics (HRA) benefits through training and communication is vital for gaining employee support and buy-in. To achieve this, organizations should provide comprehensive training sessions that explain the purpose, benefits, and processes of HRA. These sessions should highlight how HRA can improve decision-making, enhance employee development, and contribute to overall organizational success. Clear and transparent communication helps demystify HRA and addresses any misconceptions or concerns employees may have.

  Involving employees in the development and implementation of HRA practices is equally important. By seeking their input and feedback, organizations can ensure that HRA practices are fair, relevant, and aligned with employees' needs and perspectives. This collaborative approach fosters a sense of ownership and participation, making employees more likely to support and engage with HRA initiatives.

Regular updates and open forums for discussing HRA progress and insights can further enhance transparency and trust.

Overall, combining training, communication, and employee involvement creates a supportive environment for adopting HRA practices, ultimately leading to more effective and sustainable outcomes.

Strategies to Overcome Measurement Difficulties

Use a Balanced Approach

Combine quantitative and qualitative methods to assess the value of human resources. Use a balanced scorecard approach that includes financial, customer, internal process, and learning and growth perspectives to provide a comprehensive view of human capital.

Implement Technology Solutions

Implementing technology solutions can significantly enhance Human Resource Analytics (HRA) practices by improving data accuracy, accessibility, and efficiency. Leveraging advanced HR analytics tools allows organizations to collect and analyze vast amounts of data quickly and accurately. These tools can identify trends, patterns, and insights that might be missed through manual analysis, leading to more informed decision-making.

Data management systems play a crucial role in organizing and storing HR data securely. They ensure that data is easily accessible and can be retrieved when needed. These systems also facilitate data integration from various sources, providing a comprehensive view of the workforce.

Artificial intelligence (AI) can further elevate HRA practices by automating repetitive tasks, such as data entry and report generation. AI-powered algorithms can analyze complex datasets, detect anomalies, and provide predictive insights, helping HR professionals make proactive decisions. Additionally, AI can enhance employee engagement through personalized recommendations for learning and development.

By implementing these technology solutions, organizations can streamline their HRA processes, reduce the likelihood of errors, and gain deeper insights into their human capital. This technological integration supports more effective and strategic HR management, ultimately contributing to organizational success.

Standardize HRA Practices

Advocating for industry standards and guidelines in Human Resource Analytics (HRA) practices is essential to ensure consistency and comparability in measuring and reporting human capital. By developing standardized methods and metrics, organizations can achieve uniformity in their HRA approaches, allowing for more accurate benchmarking and comparison across different organizations and industries.

Standardized HRA practices help create a common framework for collecting, analyzing, and reporting HR data. This framework can include guidelines on data collection methods, key performance indicators (KPIs), and reporting formats. By adhering to these standards, organizations can ensure that their HRA practices are aligned with best practices and industry norms.

Consistency in HRA methods and metrics also facilitates better decision-making and strategic planning. When organizations use comparable metrics, they can more effectively identify trends, assess performance, and make data-driven decisions. This standardization enhances the credibility and reliability of HRA data, providing valuable insights into the workforce.

Moreover, promoting industry standards and guidelines encourages collaboration and knowledge sharing among organizations. By participating in industry forums and working groups, HR professionals can contribute to the development and refinement of HRA standards, ensuring that they reflect the evolving needs and challenges of the workforce.

In summary, standardizing HRA practices through industry standards and guidelines helps organizations achieve consistency, comparability, and reliability in measuring and reporting human capital, ultimately leading to more informed and effective HR strategies.

Engage Stakeholders

Engaging key stakeholders, including employees, managers, and accounting professionals, in the development and implementation of Human Resource Analytics (HRA) practices is crucial for enhancing their effectiveness and acceptance. Involving these stakeholders from the outset fosters a sense of ownership and collaboration, ensuring that HRA initiatives are aligned with the needs and perspectives of all parties involved.

Employees can provide valuable insights into the practicality and impact of HRA practices, helping to identify potential challenges and opportunities for improvement. Their feedback ensures that HRA initiatives are fair, transparent, and respectful of their rights, ultimately leading to greater acceptance and support.

Managers play a critical role in the implementation of HRA practices, as they are responsible for applying the insights generated by HRA to make informed decisions. By involving managers in the development process, organizations can ensure that HRA practices are relevant and practical, facilitating their integration into daily operations.

Accounting professionals bring expertise in financial reporting and metrics, helping to create frameworks that accommodate HRA data and ensure consistency in reporting. Their involvement ensures that HRA practices are aligned with financial goals and regulatory requirements, enhancing the credibility and reliability of HRA data.

Overall, engaging stakeholders in HRA initiatives helps build trust, promotes collaboration, and ensures that HRA practices are effective and widely accepted. This collaborative approach leads to more accurate and meaningful insights, ultimately driving better decision-making and organizational performance.

Continuous Improvement

To ensure Human Resource Analytics (HRA) remains effective and relevant, it's essential to adopt a mindset of continuous improvement. Regularly reviewing and updating HRA methodologies is crucial to reflect changes in the workforce, market conditions, and organizational goals. This ongoing process ensures that HRA practices stay current and can adapt to evolving circumstances.

By implementing continuous improvement processes, organizations can enhance the accuracy and relevance of their HRA practices. This involves systematically evaluating the effectiveness of current methodologies, identifying areas for improvement, and making necessary adjustments. Engaging in regular feedback loops with HR professionals, managers, and employees can provide valuable insights into the strengths and weaknesses of existing HRA practices.

Additionally, staying informed about advancements in HR technology and analytics tools can help organizations incorporate new techniques and best practices into their HRA methodologies. This proactive approach enables organizations to leverage the latest innovations to enhance data collection, analysis, and reporting.

Ultimately, committing to continuous improvement in HRA fosters a culture of learning and innovation, ensuring that organizations can effectively harness the power of analytics to drive strategic decision-making and achieve their goals.

Conclusion

Measurement difficulties in Human Resource Accounting present significant challenges, but with the right strategies, organizations can overcome these obstacles and effectively quantify the value of their human resources. By implementing a balanced approach, leveraging technology, standardizing practices, engaging stakeholders, and focusing on continuous improvement, organizations can enhance the reliability and effectiveness of their HRA initiatives. Despite challenges, the benefits of accurate and comprehensive HRA make it a valuable tool for modern organizations committed to optimizing their workforce and achieving sustainable growth.

CHAPTER NINETEEN

ETHICAL CONSIDERATIONS

Introduction to Ethical Considerations

Human Resource Accounting (HRA) involves measuring and reporting the value of human resources, and with this responsibility comes the need to uphold ethical standards. Ethical considerations in HRA ensure that practices are fair, transparent, and respectful of individuals' rights. This chapter explores the key ethical considerations in HRA and provides guidelines for maintaining ethical integrity.

Key Ethical Considerations

Data Privacy and Confidentiality

- **Consideration:** When collecting and analyzing employee data for Human Resource Analytics (HRA) purposes, privacy and confidentiality are paramount. Mishandling sensitive information can result in significant legal and ethical issues, damaging trust and exposing the organization to legal consequences.

  Firstly, organizations must establish clear policies and protocols for data collection, ensuring they comply with relevant data protection laws and regulations, such as the General Data Protection Regulation (GDPR) or the California Consumer Privacy Act (CCPA). These policies should outline the types of data collected, the purpose for which it is collected, and how it will be used, stored, and protected.

  Secondly, transparency with employees is crucial. Inform employees about what data is being collected, why it is being collected, and how it will benefit both the organization and them. This openness fosters trust and ensures employees feel respected and valued.

Thirdly, implementing robust data security measures is essential. This includes encrypting sensitive data, restricting access to authorized personnel only, and regularly reviewing and updating security protocols to protect against data breaches and cyber threats.

Lastly, regular audits and assessments of data handling practices help ensure compliance and identify potential vulnerabilities. Organizations should also provide training to HR personnel and other relevant staff on ethical data handling practices and the importance of maintaining confidentiality.

By prioritizing privacy and confidentiality, organizations can mitigate legal and ethical risks, maintain employee trust, and leverage HRA insights to drive informed and strategic decisions.

- **Guidelines:** To safeguard sensitive employee information and comply with data protection regulations, organizations must establish clear policies and procedures for data privacy and confidentiality. This includes adhering to regulations such as GDPR and CCPA by regularly reviewing and updating HR practices. Obtaining informed consent from employees before collecting their data is crucial, ensuring transparency about the purpose and use of the data. Additionally, utilizing anonymized data whenever possible helps protect employee identities and maintain confidentiality. Implementing robust security measures, providing regular training to HR personnel, and conducting audits further reinforce the organization's commitment to data privacy and confidentiality, ultimately fostering a secure and ethical work environment.

Fairness and Objectivity

- **Consideration:** Human Resource Analytics (HRA) practices must be fair and objective to prevent biases and discrimination. Ensuring that data collection and analysis methods are standardized and consistent is crucial for maintaining the credibility of HRA. Subjective evaluations can introduce personal biases, leading to unfair treatment and decisions that disproportionately affect certain groups of employees. It's essential to use objective criteria and data-driven approaches to evaluate employee performance, engagement, and other HR metrics.

Additionally, training HR personnel and managers on recognizing and mitigating biases in data interpretation and decision-making can help promote fairness. By fostering an inclusive and equitable environment, organizations can leverage HRA to make informed, unbiased decisions that support diversity and inclusion, ultimately enhancing organizational performance and employee satisfaction.

- **Guidelines:** Using standardized and objective methods for Human Resource Analytics (HRA) is vital for minimizing subjectivity and ensuring fairness. Organizations should implement structured and consistent approaches to data collection and analysis, such as using quantitative metrics and well-defined performance indicators. Incorporating multiple perspectives, like 360-degree feedback, can provide a comprehensive and unbiased view of employee performance by gathering input from peers, supervisors, subordinates, and the employees themselves. This holistic approach reduces the risk of individual biases affecting evaluations.

  It's also essential to ensure that evaluation criteria are transparent and consistently applied across the organization. Clearly defined criteria help employees understand how their performance is measured and what is expected of them. This transparency promotes trust in the evaluation process and ensures that all employees are assessed fairly and equitably. By adhering to these guidelines, organizations can leverage HRA to make informed, objective decisions that support employee development and organizational success.

Transparency and Accountability

- **Consideration:** Transparency in Human Resource Analytics (HRA) practices is vital for fostering trust among employees and stakeholders. When organizations are open about their data collection methods, analysis processes, and the purposes of using HRA, it helps build confidence and reassurance. Clearly communicating how data will be used to improve HR practices and overall organizational performance encourages employee buy-in and reduces skepticism.

  On the other hand, a lack of transparency can lead to misunderstandings and mistrust. Employees may feel uneasy about how their data is being used or fear potential misuse, leading to resistance and decreased engagement. Ensuring that HRA practices are transparent involves regularly updating employees about data usage, maintaining clear communication channels, and providing opportunities for employees to ask questions and express concerns.

By prioritizing transparency, organizations can create a culture of openness and accountability, where employees feel valued and informed. This trust fosters a positive work environment, enhances employee morale, and ultimately contributes to the organization's success.

- **Guidelines:** Clearly communicating HRA practices, policies, and criteria to employees and stakeholders is fundamental to building trust and ensuring transparency. Start by providing detailed information about the objectives, methods, and scope of HRA activities. This can be done through employee handbooks, intranet portals, and regular meetings where HRA practices are explained and discussed.

Providing regular updates and reports on HRA findings is essential for maintaining an ongoing dialogue with stakeholders. These updates should be clear, accessible, and presented in a way that highlights key insights and actions taken based on the data. Sharing both successes and areas for improvement helps demonstrate the organization's commitment to using HRA for continuous enhancement.

Holding decision-makers accountable for adhering to ethical standards in HRA practices is crucial for maintaining integrity. This involves establishing clear guidelines on ethical behavior, data privacy, and fairness, and ensuring that decision-makers are trained and aware of these standards. Regular audits and reviews can help monitor compliance and address any deviations promptly.

By following these guidelines, organizations can foster a culture of transparency, accountability, and ethical behavior in HRA, ultimately leading to more effective and trusted HR practices.

Equity and Inclusion

- **Consideration:** Promoting equity and inclusion in Human Resource Analytics (HRA) practices is essential for creating a fair and inclusive work environment. This involves ensuring that all employees are treated without discrimination and that biases in HRA are actively identified and mitigated. When biases are present in HRA practices, they can perpetuate inequality and exclusion, negatively impacting employee morale and organizational culture.

To promote equity and inclusion, organizations should implement standardized and objective methods for data collection and analysis. This helps minimize subjectivity and ensures that decisions are based on fair and consistent criteria. Additionally, incorporating diverse perspectives, such as through 360-degree feedback, can provide a more comprehensive and unbiased view of employee performance.

Training HR personnel and managers on recognizing and addressing biases is crucial for fostering an inclusive environment. By raising awareness and providing tools to mitigate biases, organizations can ensure that their HRA practices support diversity and inclusion initiatives.

Furthermore, regularly reviewing and updating HRA practices to align with best practices in equity and inclusion helps create a more equitable workplace. This continuous improvement approach ensures that HRA practices evolve to meet the needs of a diverse workforce, ultimately contributing to a more inclusive and supportive organizational culture.

- **Guidelines:** Implementing unbiased Human Resource Analytics (HRA) practices that promote diversity and inclusion is crucial for creating an equitable work environment. Organizations should use diverse data sources and perspectives to ensure a comprehensive evaluation of HR practices. This includes gathering input from various employee groups, departments, and levels to capture a broad range of experiences and viewpoints. Employing standardized and objective methods for data collection and analysis helps minimize subjectivity and biases.

Regularly reviewing HRA practices for potential biases is essential for maintaining fairness. Conducting periodic audits and assessments can help identify and address any discrepancies or biases that may arise. When biases are detected, taking corrective actions promptly is vital to ensure that HRA practices remain fair and equitable.

Training HR personnel and decision-makers on recognizing and mitigating biases further supports unbiased HRA practices. This ongoing education helps create awareness and equips staff with the tools needed to uphold ethical standards in data analysis and decision-making.

By following these guidelines, organizations can foster an inclusive and supportive work environment that values diversity and promotes equitable treatment for all employees.

Respect for Employee Rights

- **Consideration:** Human Resource Analytics (HRA) practices must prioritize respecting employees' rights, including their right to privacy, dignity, and fair treatment. Upholding these rights is essential for maintaining ethical standards and fostering a positive workplace culture. Violating these rights can result in significant ethical and legal repercussions, damaging the organization's reputation and exposing it to legal liabilities.

  Respecting employees' right to privacy involves ensuring that personal and sensitive data is collected, stored, and used responsibly. This includes obtaining informed consent from employees, clearly communicating the purpose of data collection, and implementing robust data protection measures to prevent unauthorized access and breaches.

  Upholding employees' dignity means treating them with respect and fairness throughout the HRA process. This involves avoiding intrusive or discriminatory practices, ensuring transparency in data use, and providing employees with the opportunity to access and correct their data.

  Fair treatment is crucial in HRA practices to avoid biases and discrimination. This includes using objective and standardized evaluation criteria, promoting diversity and inclusion, and ensuring that all employees are assessed equitably.

  By prioritizing these considerations, organizations can create a trustworthy and ethical HRA environment that respects employees' rights, enhances employee morale, and supports overall organizational success.

- **Guidelines:** To ensure fair and ethical Human Resource Analytics (HRA) practices, it is essential to comply with labor laws and regulations, respecting employees' rights to access their data and provide feedback on their evaluations. This includes establishing transparent procedures for employees to review and correct their personal information. Additionally, addressing employee concerns and grievances related to HRA practices promptly and fairly fosters trust and demonstrates the organization's commitment to ethical standards. By adhering to these guidelines, organizations can create a trustworthy and accountable HRA environment that supports employee satisfaction and overall organizational success.

Ethical Guidelines for HRA Practices

Informed Consent

Obtaining informed consent from employees is a critical aspect of ethical Human Resource Analytics (HRA) practices. Before collecting and analyzing their data, it's essential to clearly explain to employees the purpose, scope, and intended use of the data. This transparency helps employees understand why their data is being collected and how it will benefit both them and the organization.

The informed consent process should include providing detailed information about the types of data being collected, the methods used for data collection, how the data will be analyzed, and how the findings will be applied. It is important to communicate any potential risks and benefits associated with data collection and usage. This comprehensive explanation ensures that employees can make an informed decision about their participation.

Additionally, organizations must respect employees' rights by giving them the option to opt out of data collection and analysis if they choose. This voluntary participation ensures that employees feel respected and valued, and it helps build trust between the organization and its workforce.

By prioritizing informed consent, organizations can uphold ethical standards, protect employees' privacy and dignity, and foster a positive and transparent workplace culture.

Data Security

To safeguard employee data, it is essential to implement robust data security measures that protect against unauthorized access, breaches, and misuse. Regularly reviewing and updating data security protocols helps address emerging threats and ensures that data protection measures remain effective. Encryption, strict access controls, and regular security audits are key components of a comprehensive data security strategy. Additionally, ongoing security training for employees and maintaining an incident response plan are critical for mitigating risks and responding promptly to potential security incidents. Prioritizing data security not only ensures compliance with data protection regulations but also fosters a secure and trustworthy work environment.

Transparency in Communication

Effectively communicating HRA practices, policies, and criteria to employees and stakeholders is essential for building trust and ensuring transparency. Organizations should provide clear explanations of how data is collected, analyzed, and utilized in decision-making processes. This involves detailing the objectives and scope of HRA activities, the methods used for data collection and analysis, and how the insights derived from HRA are applied to improve HR practices and organizational performance. Transparent communication helps employees understand the value and purpose of HRA, fostering a sense of inclusion and cooperation. By keeping all stakeholders informed, organizations can create a culture of openness and accountability, ultimately enhancing the effectiveness of HRA practices.

Regular Ethical Audits

Conducting regular ethical audits of HRA practices is crucial for identifying and addressing potential ethical issues. These audits help ensure that data collection and analysis methods align with ethical standards and organizational values. Involving independent auditors or ethics committees in the audit process promotes impartiality and accountability, providing an unbiased assessment of HRA practices. Regular ethical audits not only highlight areas for improvement but also reinforce the organization's commitment to ethical behavior and transparency. By proactively addressing ethical concerns, organizations can maintain the integrity of their HRA practices and build trust with employees and stakeholders.

Training and Awareness

Providing training and awareness programs for HR professionals and managers on ethical considerations in Human Resource Analytics (HRA) is essential. These programs should cover the importance of ethical practices and equip HR personnel with the knowledge and skills to uphold ethical standards. Regular training sessions help raise awareness about potential ethical issues, such as biases and data privacy concerns, and provide guidance on how to address them. By fostering a culture of ethical behavior, organizations can ensure that HRA practices are conducted responsibly, maintaining trust and integrity in their HR functions.

Employee Involvement

Involving employees in the development and implementation of Human Resource Analytics (HRA) practices is vital for ensuring fairness, transparency, and respect for their rights. By seeking their input and feedback, organizations can create HRA practices that are more aligned with employees' needs and perspectives. This inclusive approach not only enhances the credibility and effectiveness of HRA but also fosters a sense of ownership and collaboration. Regularly engaging employees through surveys, focus groups, and open forums allows them to voice their opinions and contribute to the design and refinement of HRA practices. This collaborative effort helps build trust and ensures that HRA practices are implemented in a way that respects employees' rights and promotes a positive organizational culture.

Case Studies and Examples

- **Infosys Limited:** Infosys upholds ethical standards in its HRA practices by ensuring data privacy, transparency, and fairness. The company regularly communicates its HRA policies and criteria to employees and stakeholders, building trust and accountability.
- **Tata Consultancy Services (TCS):** TCS promotes equity and inclusion in its HRA practices by implementing unbiased evaluation methods and ensuring diverse perspectives. The company conducts regular ethical audits to identify and address potential ethical issues.

Conclusion

Ethical considerations are paramount in Human Resource Accounting to ensure fair, transparent, and respectful practices. By upholding ethical standards, organizations can build trust, promote equity and inclusion, and protect employees' rights. Implementing robust ethical guidelines and regularly reviewing HRA practices are essential for maintaining ethical integrity and achieving sustainable organizational success.

CHAPTER TWENTY

IMPLEMENTATION CHALLENGES

Introduction to Implementation Challenges

Implementing Human Resource Accounting (HRA) in an organization can be a complex and challenging process. Despite the benefits of accurately measuring and reporting the value of human resources, several obstacles can hinder the successful adoption and execution of HRA practices. This chapter explores the key implementation challenges in HRA and provides strategies to address them.

Key Implementation Challenges

Lack of Awareness and Understanding

- **Challenge:** Many organizations and HR professionals may lack awareness and understanding of HRA concepts, methods, and benefits. This can lead to resistance to adopting HRA practices.
- **Strategy:** Conduct training and awareness programs for HR professionals, managers, and key stakeholders to educate them about the importance and benefits of HRA. Use case studies and real-life examples to illustrate the value of HRA.

Data Collection and Management

- **Challenge:** Accurate and comprehensive data collection is critical for HRA, but it can be difficult to obtain and manage. Incomplete or inaccurate data can undermine the effectiveness of HRA.
- **Strategy:** Implement robust data collection and management systems to ensure data accuracy and completeness. Use technology, such as HR

analytics tools, to streamline data collection and analysis. Regularly review and update data sources to maintain data integrity.

Integration with Existing Systems

- **Challenge:** Integrating HRA practices with existing HR and financial systems can be complex and time-consuming. Inconsistent data formats and systems can create obstacles to seamless integration.
- **Strategy:** Work closely with IT and finance departments to develop integrated reporting systems that combine HRA data with existing HR and financial data. Use middleware and data integration tools to ensure consistency and compatibility.

Standardization and Consistency

- **Challenge:** The lack of standardized methods and practices for HRA can result in inconsistencies in measurement and reporting. This makes it difficult to compare HRA data across different departments or organizations.
- **Strategy:** Advocate for industry standards and guidelines for HRA practices. Develop and implement standardized methods and metrics within the organization to ensure consistency and comparability.

Resource Constraints

- **Challenge:** Implementing HRA can require significant investment in terms of time, money, and personnel. Smaller organizations may find it challenging to allocate resources for HRA initiatives.
- **Strategy:** Prioritize key HRA initiatives that align with organizational goals and provide the most value. Consider outsourcing certain HRA functions to specialized firms or consultants to reduce costs and resource constraints.

Employee Privacy and Confidentiality

- **Challenge:** Collecting and analyzing employee data for HRA purposes raises concerns about privacy and confidentiality. Inappropriate handling of sensitive data can lead to legal and ethical issues.

- **Strategy:** Establish clear policies and procedures for data privacy and confidentiality. Ensure compliance with data protection regulations and obtain informed consent from employees for data collection. Use anonymized data where possible to protect employee privacy.

Resistance to Change

- **Challenge:** Organizations and employees may resist adopting HRA practices due to a lack of understanding, fear of change, or concerns about the implications of being evaluated.
- **Strategy:** Promote awareness and understanding of HRA benefits through communication and engagement. Involve employees in the development and implementation of HRA practices to gain their support and buy-in. Address concerns and provide support to ease the transition.

Strategies to Overcome Implementation Challenges
Leadership Support
Obtain strong support from organizational leadership to champion HRA initiatives. Leadership endorsement can drive the adoption of HRA practices and allocate necessary resources.
Clear Communication
Communicate the objectives, benefits, and processes of HRA clearly to all stakeholders. Use regular updates, workshops, and informational sessions to keep everyone informed and engaged.
Pilot Programs
Implement pilot programs to test HRA practices on a smaller scale before full-scale deployment. Use pilot results to identify potential issues, gather feedback, and make necessary adjustments.
Collaboration and Cross-Functional Teams
Form cross-functional teams involving HR, finance, IT, and other relevant departments to collaborate on HRA implementation. Leverage the expertise of different functions to ensure a holistic approach.
Continuous Improvement
Regularly review and evaluate HRA practices to identify areas for improvement. Implement feedback loops to gather input from employees and stakeholders, and continuously refine HRA methodologies.
Case Studies and Examples

- **Infosys Limited:** Infosys successfully implemented HRA by securing leadership support, conducting training programs, and leveraging technology for data collection and analysis. The company's integrated reporting system combines HRA data with financial data, providing comprehensive insights.
- **Tata Consultancy Services (TCS):** TCS overcame implementation challenges by forming cross-functional teams and using pilot programs to test HRA practices. The company's commitment to data privacy and transparency has built trust among employees and stakeholders.

Conclusion

Implementing Human Resource Accounting presents several challenges, but with the right strategies, organizations can overcome these obstacles and successfully adopt HRA practices. By securing leadership support, promoting awareness, leveraging technology, and prioritizing key initiatives, organizations can enhance the effectiveness of HRA and achieve sustainable growth. Despite challenges, the benefits of accurate and comprehensive HRA make it a valuable tool for modern organizations committed to optimizing their workforce.

CHAPTER TWENTY-ONE

HUMAN RESOURCE AUDIT

Introduction to Human Resource Audit

A Human Resource (HR) Audit is a comprehensive evaluation of an organization's HR policies, practices, systems, and procedures. The primary objective of an HR Audit is to identify strengths and weaknesses in the HR function, ensure compliance with legal and regulatory requirements, and recommend improvements to enhance overall organizational performance. This chapter explores the key aspects of HR Audit, its importance, and best practices for conducting effective audits.

Importance of Human Resource Audit

- **Compliance and Risk Management:** HR audits play a critical role in ensuring that an organization's HR practices comply with legal and regulatory requirements, thereby reducing the risk of legal issues and potential penalties. By systematically reviewing HR policies, procedures, and practices, audits help identify areas of non-compliance and gaps that could expose the organization to legal risks. This proactive approach allows organizations to address these issues before they escalate into legal challenges, fines, or reputational damage. Additionally, HR audits provide a framework for continuous monitoring and improvement, ensuring that HR practices remain aligned with current laws and regulations. Ultimately, this fosters a compliant and legally sound HR environment, supporting the organization's overall risk management strategy.

- **Strategic Alignment:** HR audits are invaluable for ensuring that HR practices are strategically aligned with the organization's goals and mission. By thoroughly reviewing HR policies, procedures, and activities, audits help identify areas where HR functions may not fully support the organization's strategic objectives. This alignment is crucial as it ensures that HR initiatives, such as talent acquisition, employee development, and performance management, are effectively contributing to the overall success of the organization. Additionally, aligning HR practices with organizational strategies helps create a cohesive and motivated workforce, fosters a positive work culture, and enhances the organization's ability to achieve its long-term goals. Through regular HR audits, organizations can continuously refine their HR functions to stay in sync with evolving strategic priorities, thereby driving sustained growth and success.

- **Employee Engagement and Satisfaction:** Employee engagement and satisfaction are critical indicators of organizational health and performance. Audits that assess these factors provide valuable insights into how employees perceive their work environment, management, and overall job satisfaction. By gathering data through surveys, interviews, and focus groups, organizations can identify key drivers of engagement and areas where improvements are needed.

  These audits can reveal issues such as lack of recognition, insufficient career development opportunities, or poor work-life balance that may be impacting employee morale. By addressing these areas, organizations can implement targeted initiatives to enhance the employee experience, such as creating more recognition programs, offering professional development opportunities, or improving workplace policies.

  Improving employee engagement and satisfaction not only boosts morale but also leads to higher productivity, reduced turnover, and a stronger organizational culture. Regularly assessing and addressing these factors ensures that employees feel valued, supported, and motivated to contribute to the organization's success.

- **Cost Management:** Cost management is a crucial aspect of HR practices, and identifying inefficiencies and redundancies can lead to significant cost savings and better resource allocation. By conducting a thorough analysis of HR processes, organizations can pinpoint areas where resources are being wasted or where processes are duplicated. This includes examining recruitment strategies, training programs, administrative tasks, and technology use.

For instance, streamlining recruitment processes can reduce the time and cost associated with hiring new employees. Implementing more efficient training programs can minimize training expenses while still enhancing employee skills. Automating administrative tasks through HR Information Systems (HRIS) can reduce manual labor and associated costs.

Additionally, optimizing benefit packages and compensation structures can ensure that the organization is providing competitive and fair compensation without overspending. By reallocating resources to more strategic initiatives, organizations can improve overall efficiency, reduce costs, and enhance the effectiveness of HR functions.

Ultimately, effective cost management in HR practices leads to better financial health for the organization and the ability to invest in areas that drive growth and innovation.

- **Benchmarking:** Benchmarking in HR audits is an essential practice that allows organizations to compare their HR policies, procedures, and performance metrics against industry standards and best practices. By doing so, organizations can identify gaps and areas for improvement, ensuring they remain competitive in attracting, retaining, and developing talent.

  This process involves collecting data from similar organizations within the same industry or sector and comparing key HR metrics such as employee turnover rates, time-to-hire, training effectiveness, and employee satisfaction levels. Benchmarking provides a clear picture of where an organization stands in relation to its peers and highlights opportunities to adopt more effective practices.

  By leveraging benchmarking insights, organizations can implement targeted improvements, align their HR strategies with industry trends, and ultimately enhance their overall performance. This proactive approach not only helps in maintaining competitiveness but also fosters a culture of continuous improvement and excellence within the organization.

Key Components of a Human Resource Audit
HR Policies and Procedures

- Evaluate the organization's HR policies and procedures to ensure they are up-to-date, compliant with legal requirements, and aligned with organizational goals.

- Assess the effectiveness of policies related to recruitment, selection, training, performance management, compensation, benefits, and employee relations.

Compliance and Legal Issues

- Review HR practices to ensure compliance with labor laws, employment regulations, and industry standards.
- Identify potential legal risks and recommend corrective actions to mitigate these risks.

Recruitment and Selection

- Assess the effectiveness of recruitment and selection processes, including job analysis, sourcing, interviewing, and hiring practices.
- Evaluate the organization's ability to attract and retain top talent.

Training and Development

- Review training and development programs to ensure they meet the needs of employees and the organization.
- Assess the effectiveness of training initiatives in enhancing employee skills and performance.

Performance Management

- Evaluate the organization's performance management system, including goal setting, performance appraisal, feedback, and development plans.
- Identify areas for improvement to ensure fair and effective performance evaluations.

Compensation and Benefits

- Assess the competitiveness and fairness of the organization's compensation and benefits packages.
- Review pay structures, incentive programs, and benefits offerings to ensure they align with industry standards and employee needs.

Employee Relations

- Review employee relations practices, including grievance handling, conflict resolution, and communication channels.
- Assess the organization's efforts to foster a positive and inclusive work environment.

HR Information Systems (HRIS)

- Evaluate the effectiveness of HR information systems in managing and processing HR data.
- Assess data accuracy, accessibility, and security to ensure effective HR operations.

Steps in Conducting a Human Resource Audit
Planning and Preparation

- Define the scope and objectives of the audit.
- Assemble an audit team with relevant expertise.
- Develop an audit plan and timeline, outlining the key areas to be audited and the methods to be used.

Data Collection

- Gather relevant data through various methods, such as document reviews, surveys, interviews, and observations.
- Collect data on HR policies, procedures, practices, and employee feedback.

Analysis and Evaluation

- Analyze the collected data to identify strengths, weaknesses, compliance issues, and areas for improvement.
- Compare the organization's HR practices against industry standards and best practices.

Reporting and Recommendations

- Prepare an audit report summarizing the findings, including strengths, weaknesses, compliance issues, and recommendations for improvement.
- Present the report to key stakeholders, including HR leadership and senior management.

Implementation and Follow-Up

- Develop an action plan to implement the recommended improvements.
- Monitor progress and conduct follow-up audits to ensure that corrective actions have been taken and improvements have been achieved.

Best Practices for Human Resource Audit

- **Involve Key Stakeholders:** Engaging key stakeholders in the HR audit process is essential for ensuring buy-in and support for the findings and recommendations. This involves actively involving HR leadership, managers, and employees at various stages of the audit to create a sense of ownership and collaboration.

  By involving HR leadership in defining the scope and objectives of the audit, their insights and strategic perspective help align the audit with organizational goals. Engaging managers during data collection and analysis allows them to contribute their firsthand knowledge of HR practices and employee experiences, providing a comprehensive understanding of the current state of HR functions. Additionally, including employees through surveys, focus groups, and interviews demonstrates that their opinions are valued and considered in decision-making.

  Maintaining open and transparent communication with all stakeholders throughout the audit process is crucial. Regular updates, meetings, and feedback sessions help build trust and ensure alignment with the audit's objectives and outcomes. This collaborative approach fosters a sense of responsibility and accountability among all involved, making the implementation of recommendations more effective.

  Ultimately, involving key stakeholders in the HR audit process enhances the overall success of the audit and supports continuous improvement, leading to more effective HR practices and a stronger organizational culture.

- **Maintain Objectivity:** Maintaining objectivity in the audit process is crucial to ensure the findings and recommendations are unbiased and credible. To achieve this, it's important that the audit team remains independent and free from any conflicts of interest. An impartial audit team can objectively assess HR practices without being influenced by internal dynamics or relationships within the organization.

  Consider using external auditors or consultants for an impartial assessment. External auditors bring a fresh perspective and are not affected by internal biases. Their independence helps provide a more accurate and reliable evaluation of HR practices.

  Implementing strict confidentiality protocols is essential to protect the integrity of the audit process. Auditors should have access to all necessary information while ensuring that sensitive data is handled with care and confidentiality.

  By maintaining objectivity and using external auditors or consultants, organizations can ensure that their audits provide valuable insights for improving HR practices and achieving organizational goals.

- **Use Multiple Data Sources:** Collecting data from multiple sources, such as documents, surveys, interviews, and observations, is essential for obtaining a comprehensive view of HR practices. Documents like HR policies, employee handbooks, performance reports, and compliance records offer a baseline understanding of formal practices. Surveys provide quantitative data on employee perceptions, satisfaction, and engagement, highlighting trends and areas for improvement. Interviews with employees, managers, and HR personnel offer qualitative insights and deeper context to survey results, uncovering underlying issues. Observations of HR activities and processes, such as recruitment, training sessions, and performance appraisals, provide firsthand insights into how practices are implemented and experienced. By triangulating data from these diverse sources, organizations can create a well-rounded assessment of their HR functions, identify strengths and weaknesses, and develop effective improvement strategies. This multi-faceted approach ensures a thorough and accurate evaluation, ultimately enhancing HR practices and overall organizational performance.

- **Focus on Continuous Improvement:** Viewing the HR audit process as an opportunity for continuous improvement rather than a one-time assessment is crucial for maintaining and enhancing the effectiveness of HR practices. By implementing regular audits, organizations can continuously monitor progress, identify new areas for improvement, and adapt to changing regulations and organizational needs. This proactive approach ensures that HR practices remain relevant, efficient, and aligned with strategic goals.

Regular audits provide a framework for ongoing evaluation and refinement, enabling organizations to address emerging issues before they become significant problems. This iterative process fosters a culture of continuous improvement, where feedback and data from each audit cycle are used to drive enhancements in HR policies, procedures, and practices.

Moreover, continuous audits help track the effectiveness of implemented changes, providing valuable insights into their impact on employee satisfaction, performance, and overall organizational success. This approach ensures that HR functions evolve in response to internal and external developments, supporting the long-term growth and sustainability of the organization.

By prioritizing continuous improvement through regular HR audits, organizations can achieve higher levels of efficiency, compliance, and employee engagement, ultimately contributing to a more robust and dynamic workplace.

- **Communicate Transparently:** Communicating transparently during the HR audit process is essential for fostering trust and ensuring stakeholder buy-in. Begin by clearly articulating the audit's purpose, scope, and objectives to all relevant stakeholders, including HR leadership, managers, and employees. This initial communication helps set expectations and provides a clear understanding of the audit's goals.

  Once the audit is underway, keep stakeholders informed about the progress and any preliminary findings. Regular updates through meetings, emails, or reports maintain engagement and demonstrate the organization's commitment to transparency. After the audit is completed, present the findings and recommendations in a straightforward and accessible manner. Use clear language, supported by data visualizations if necessary, to make the information understandable.

  Finally, provide regular updates on the progress of implementing the recommended improvements. This can include sharing milestones achieved, addressing any challenges encountered, and outlining the next steps. Continuous communication ensures that stakeholders remain informed and involved, fostering a collaborative environment where everyone works together to enhance HR practices and achieve organizational goals.

Case Studies and Examples

- **Infosys Limited:** Infosys conducts regular HR audits to ensure compliance, identify areas for improvement, and align HR practices with organizational goals. The company's commitment to continuous improvement has resulted in enhanced HR efficiency and employee satisfaction.
- **Tata Consultancy Services (TCS):** TCS uses HR audits to benchmark its HR practices against industry standards and identify best practices. The company's focus on data-driven audits has led to improved HR performance and strategic alignment.

Conclusion

A Human Resource Audit is a valuable tool for evaluating and improving an organization's HR policies, practices, and systems. By conducting regular audits, organizations can ensure compliance, enhance performance, and align HR practices with strategic goals. Despite challenges, the benefits of a well-executed HR audit make it an essential practice for modern organizations committed to optimizing their workforce and achieving sustainable growth.

CHAPTER TWENTY-TWO

CONCEPT AND SCOPE

Introduction to Human Resource Accounting (HRA)

Human Resource Accounting (HRA) is a specialized area of accounting that focuses on identifying, measuring, and reporting the value of human resources within an organization. HRA seeks to quantify the economic contributions of employees and integrate this information into financial statements to provide a more comprehensive view of an organization's assets and performance. By recognizing the value of human capital, HRA aims to enhance decision-making, strategic planning, and overall organizational effectiveness.

Concept of Human Resource Accounting

- **Definition:** Human Resource Accounting (HRA) is the process of identifying, measuring, and reporting the economic value of an organization's human resources. It involves quantifying the financial worth of employees' skills, knowledge, and abilities, and incorporating this value into the organization's financial statements.

- **Purpose:** The primary purpose of HRA is to provide a more accurate representation of an organization's assets by including the value of human resources. This information helps stakeholders make informed decisions about resource allocation, investment in employee development, and overall strategic planning.

- **Key Elements:** HRA focuses on several key elements, including the cost of acquiring and developing human resources, the value of employees' contributions, and the potential future economic benefits generated by human capital. It considers both tangible and intangible aspects of human resources, such as skills, knowledge, experience, and potential for growth.

- **Measurement Methods:** Various methods are used to measure the value of human resources, including cost-based approaches (e.g., historical cost, replacement cost) and value-based approaches (e.g., present value of future earnings, economic value added). These methods provide different perspectives on the financial worth of human capital.

Scope of Human Resource Accounting

The scope of HRA encompasses a wide range of activities and applications, including:

- **Measurement and Valuation of Human Resources:** HRA involves quantifying the economic value of employees through various measurement and valuation methods. This includes assessing the costs associated with recruitment, training, and development, as well as evaluating the potential future contributions of employees.
- **Integration with Financial Reporting:** HRA aims to integrate the value of human resources into traditional financial statements. This provides stakeholders with a more comprehensive view of an organization's assets and performance, enhancing transparency and accountability.
- **Strategic Human Resource Management (HRM):** HRA supports strategic HRM by providing data-driven insights into workforce trends, skills gaps, and potential areas for investment. This information helps organizations align their HR practices with overall strategic goals and make informed decisions about talent management.
- **Performance Evaluation and Management:** HRA offers a framework for evaluating employee performance and contributions. By measuring the economic value generated by human resources, organizations can assess the effectiveness of their HR policies and practices and identify areas for improvement.
- **Resource Allocation and Investment:** HRA helps organizations allocate resources effectively by quantifying the costs and benefits associated with human resources. This information supports decisions about investment in employee development, training programs, and other HR initiatives.
- **Compliance and Risk Management:** HRA ensures that HR practices comply with legal and regulatory requirements, reducing the risk of legal issues and penalties. It also helps organizations identify and address potential HR-related risks, such as workforce shortages or skill gaps.

- **Employee Engagement and Retention:** HRA provides insights into employee engagement and satisfaction levels, helping organizations implement initiatives to enhance the employee experience and reduce turnover.

Benefits of Human Resource Accounting

- **Enhanced Decision-Making:** HRA provides valuable data for informed decision-making about HR practices, resource allocation, and strategic planning.
- **Improved Financial Reporting:** By including the value of human resources in financial statements, HRA offers a more accurate representation of an organization's assets and performance.
- **Increased Accountability:** HRA highlights the importance of human capital and encourages organizations to invest in employee development and retention.
- **Greater Transparency:** HRA enhances transparency in reporting by providing stakeholders with a comprehensive view of the organization's human capital and its impact on performance.
- **Competitive Advantage:** Organizations that effectively manage and value their human resources can achieve a competitive edge in the market.

Challenges and Limitations

Despite its benefits, HRA faces several challenges and limitations, including:

- **Data Availability and Accuracy:** Accurate and comprehensive data on employee performance, skills, and potential can be difficult to obtain and measure.
- **Subjectivity and Bias:** Valuing human resources involves subjective estimates and judgments, which can introduce biases and inconsistencies.
- **Lack of Standardization:** The lack of standardized methods and practices for HRA can result in variations in measurement and reporting.
- **Cost and Complexity:** Implementing HRA can be expensive and time-consuming, requiring significant investment in data collection, analysis, and reporting.

Conclusion

Human Resource Accounting is a valuable tool for recognizing and quantifying the economic value of an organization's human resources. By integrating the value of human capital into financial reporting and strategic planning, HRA enhances decision-making, transparency, and overall organizational performance. Despite challenges, the benefits of HRA make it a crucial practice for modern organizations committed to optimizing their workforce and achieving sustainable growth.

CHAPTER TWENTY-THREE

AUDIT PROCESS

Introduction to the HR Audit Process

The Human Resource (HR) Audit is a systematic and comprehensive evaluation of an organization's HR policies, practices, systems, and procedures. The primary objective of an HR Audit is to identify strengths and weaknesses in the HR function, ensure compliance with legal and regulatory requirements, and recommend improvements to enhance overall organizational performance. This chapter outlines the detailed steps involved in the HR Audit process.

Steps in the HR Audit Process
Planning and Preparation

- **Define Objectives:** Establishing clear objectives and scope is critical for the success of an HR audit. These objectives typically include ensuring compliance with legal and regulatory requirements, identifying areas for performance improvement, aligning HR practices with the organization's strategic goals, and managing HR-related risks. By defining these objectives, organizations can focus their audit efforts on specific areas, leading to more targeted and actionable findings. This clarity also helps allocate resources effectively, ensuring that the audit delivers valuable insights for continuous improvement. Overall, a well-defined audit scope enhances the effectiveness of the HR function, supports organizational success, and fosters a culture of continuous improvement.

- **Select Audit Team:** Assembling a proficient audit team is crucial for a successful HR audit. The team should comprise individuals with diverse expertise, including HR professionals, auditors, and, if necessary, external consultants. HR professionals bring valuable insights into the organization's policies and practices, while auditors offer an objective perspective and ensure that the audit adheres to established standards. External consultants can provide specialized knowledge and an unbiased viewpoint, enhancing the audit's effectiveness. By selecting a team with the right mix of skills and experience, organizations can ensure a thorough and accurate assessment of their HR function, leading to actionable recommendations for improvement.

- **Develop Audit Plan:** Developing a comprehensive audit plan is essential for a successful HR audit. This plan should outline the key areas to be audited, such as recruitment, compensation, performance management, and compliance with legal regulations. It should specify the methods to be used, including document reviews, interviews, surveys, and data analysis. The timeline for each audit phase, from initial planning to final reporting, should be clearly defined to ensure the audit stays on track. Additionally, the plan should detail the resources required, such as the audit team members, tools, and any external consultants. A well-structured audit plan ensures a thorough and efficient audit process, leading to actionable insights and improvements in HR practices.

Data Collection

- **Document Review:** Document review is a fundamental component of HR audits, involving the systematic collection and examination of various key documents. This process includes reviewing HR policies and procedures to ensure they are up-to-date and compliant with legal standards. Employee handbooks are also assessed to confirm they clearly communicate company policies and expectations. Job descriptions are examined for accuracy and alignment with organizational goals. Training materials are reviewed to evaluate the effectiveness of employee development programs. Performance appraisal forms are analyzed to identify strengths and weaknesses in performance management. Finally, compliance records are scrutinized to ensure adherence to legal and regulatory requirements. This thorough review provides critical insights into the effectiveness and compliance of HR practices, guiding strategic improvements.
- **Surveys and Questionnaires:** Conducting surveys and questionnaires is a vital step in HR audits for gathering diverse perspectives on HR practices and issues. By collecting input from employees, managers, and

other stakeholders, organizations can gain valuable insights into the effectiveness and impact of their HR initiatives. Surveys and questionnaires can cover various topics, such as employee satisfaction, engagement, training effectiveness, performance management, and workplace culture. This data helps identify strengths, weaknesses, and areas for improvement, enabling organizations to make informed decisions and implement targeted strategies. Additionally, involving stakeholders in the audit process fosters a sense of inclusion and transparency, promoting a positive organizational culture and enhancing overall employee engagement.

- **Interviews:** Conducting interviews with key stakeholders is a vital aspect of the HR audit process. These interviews involve direct, in-depth conversations with HR leaders, managers, and employees to gather qualitative insights into HR practices, policies, and overall organizational culture. By engaging with these individuals, auditors can gain a deeper understanding of how HR initiatives are perceived and experienced at different levels of the organization.

  Interviews provide an opportunity to explore specific issues in detail, uncover hidden challenges, and identify areas for improvement that may not be evident through document reviews or surveys alone. HR leaders can offer insights into strategic goals and the alignment of HR practices, while managers can share their experiences with talent management, performance appraisals, and day-to-day HR operations. Employees, on the other hand, can provide valuable feedback on their experiences, engagement levels, and satisfaction with HR policies and programs.

  The qualitative data collected through interviews complements the quantitative data from surveys and questionnaires, providing a comprehensive view of the organization's HR function. This holistic approach enables auditors to develop more targeted and effective recommendations for enhancing HR practices, fostering a positive work environment, and ultimately contributing to organizational success.

- **Observations:** Observing HR processes and activities is a crucial component of HR audits. This involves directly witnessing various HR functions, such as recruitment, onboarding, training sessions, and performance reviews, to evaluate their effectiveness and compliance with established policies and regulations. By observing these activities in real-time, auditors can gain a first-hand understanding of how HR practices are implemented and identify any potential gaps or inefficiencies.

For instance, during recruitment and onboarding, auditors can assess whether the procedures align with best practices, ensure a positive candidate experience, and comply with legal requirements. Observing training sessions allows auditors to evaluate the relevance and impact of the training programs on employee development and performance. Similarly, by witnessing performance reviews, auditors can determine if the process is fair, consistent, and effectively supports employee growth.

These observations provide valuable qualitative data that complement other audit methods, such as document reviews and interviews. The insights gained help organizations refine their HR practices, enhance operational efficiency, and ensure a positive and compliant work environment.

Analysis and Evaluation

- **Benchmarking:** Benchmarking is a key component of HR audits that involves comparing an organization's HR practices against industry standards and best practices. This process helps identify gaps and areas for improvement, ensuring that the organization remains competitive and up-to-date with evolving HR trends.

  By analyzing data from similar organizations, HR audits can highlight differences in recruitment strategies, employee engagement initiatives, performance management systems, and compensation structures. This comparison provides valuable insights into what works well in other organizations and where your organization may be falling short.

  Implementing best practices identified through benchmarking can lead to significant enhancements in HR functions, such as improved employee satisfaction, higher retention rates, and more effective talent management. Ultimately, benchmarking helps organizations continuously refine their HR practices, driving overall performance and success.

- **Compliance Check:** A compliance check is a critical aspect of HR audits that involves assessing the organization's HR practices to ensure they adhere to labor laws, employment regulations, and industry standards. This process helps identify potential legal risks and ensures that the organization maintains a fair and legally compliant work environment.

During a compliance check, auditors review various HR policies and procedures, such as hiring practices, compensation structures, employee benefits, workplace safety, and termination processes. They compare these practices against relevant legal requirements and industry standards to identify any discrepancies or areas of non-compliance.

For example, auditors may examine whether the organization complies with minimum wage laws, overtime regulations, anti-discrimination policies, and health and safety standards. They may also assess compliance with employee rights related to leave, working hours, and workplace accommodations.

By identifying potential legal risks, auditors can provide recommendations for corrective actions, such as updating policies, providing additional training, or implementing more robust compliance monitoring systems. These actions help mitigate legal risks, avoid potential fines and penalties, and create a more transparent and accountable HR function.

Overall, a thorough compliance check ensures that the organization's HR practices are legally sound and aligned with industry standards, fostering a positive and compliant work environment.

- **Performance Assessment:** Performance assessment is a critical component of HR audits, focusing on evaluating the effectiveness of HR practices in achieving organizational goals, enhancing employee performance, and fostering a positive work environment. This involves a comprehensive review of various HR processes and their impact on the organization.

  By examining performance management systems, auditors can assess whether they effectively set clear expectations, provide constructive feedback, and support employee development. This includes evaluating the effectiveness of performance appraisals, goal-setting processes, and feedback mechanisms in driving employee performance and motivation.

  Additionally, auditors review how well HR practices align with organizational goals, such as talent acquisition strategies, training and development programs, and succession planning. By ensuring that these initiatives support the organization's strategic objectives, HR can contribute more effectively to overall business success.

- **Data Analysis:** Data analysis is a critical step in the HR audit process, as it involves examining the collected data to uncover valuable insights. By analyzing quantitative and qualitative data from surveys, interviews, document reviews, and observations, auditors can identify patterns and trends that reveal the overall health of the HR function.

For instance, data analysis can highlight recurring issues in employee satisfaction, such as consistent concerns about work-life balance or career development opportunities. By identifying these patterns, organizations can implement targeted interventions to address the root causes.

Trends in workforce metrics, such as turnover rates or absenteeism, can also be analyzed to understand underlying factors and predict future challenges. This helps organizations proactively manage workforce planning and retention strategies.

Additionally, data analysis reveals strengths and weaknesses in HR practices, providing a clear picture of what is working well and areas that require improvement. For example, if training programs are shown to have a positive impact on employee performance, the organization can invest more in these initiatives. Conversely, if performance appraisals are found to be inconsistent or ineffective, they can be redesigned to enhance their impact.

Reporting and Recommendations

- **Prepare Audit Report:** Compiling a comprehensive audit report involves gathering all findings and presenting them in a structured format. The report should start with an executive summary that provides a high-level overview of the audit's objectives, scope, and key findings. This is followed by a detailed analysis, which delves into the specific data and insights obtained from document reviews, surveys, interviews, and observations. The report should clearly outline the organization's strengths, highlighting areas where HR practices are effective and aligned with best practices. It should also identify weaknesses, pinpointing gaps or inefficiencies that need to be addressed. Additionally, the report must document any compliance issues, specifying areas where the organization may not be adhering to legal or regulatory requirements. Finally, the report should offer actionable recommendations for improvement, prioritizing them based on their impact and feasibility, to guide the organization in enhancing its HR practices and overall performance.

- **Present Findings:** Presenting the audit report to key stakeholders, including HR leadership, senior management, and the board of directors, is a crucial step in the HR audit process. The presentation should start with an executive summary that provides a high-level overview of the audit's objectives, scope, and key findings. This is followed by highlighting the most significant findings, including both strengths and weaknesses in HR practices, along with any compliance issues identified. It's important to use clear and concise language, supported by data visualizations, to make the findings easily understandable. The presentation should also include actionable recommendations for addressing identified issues, prioritized based on their impact and feasibility. Concluding with a Q&A session allows stakeholders to seek clarification and discuss the proposed actions, ensuring a comprehensive understanding of the audit's implications and fostering informed decision-making for continuous improvement.

- **Action Plan:** An effective action plan is essential for implementing the recommended improvements identified during an HR audit. This plan should detail specific steps to address the findings, including establishing clear timelines for each initiative to ensure progress is monitored and milestones are met. Responsibilities should be assigned to individuals or teams, clearly defining their roles and expectations to ensure accountability. Additionally, the action plan should identify the resources needed, such as budget allocations, staff, or expertise, to support successful implementation. By creating a well-structured action plan, organizations can ensure that the recommended improvements are effectively carried out, leading to enhanced HR practices and overall organizational success.

Implementation and Follow-Up

- **Implement Recommendations:** Implementing recommendations is a crucial step in the HR audit process. It involves executing the action plan to carry out the improvements identified during the audit. This requires ensuring that the necessary resources and support are available to make the changes effectively.

    First, it's important to allocate the required resources, such as budget, personnel, and tools, to support the implementation of the recommended improvements. This may involve securing additional funding, hiring new staff, or investing in new technology to streamline HR processes.

Next, clearly communicate the action plan to all stakeholders involved, including HR professionals, managers, and employees. Ensure that everyone understands their roles and responsibilities in implementing the changes. Providing training and support can help employees adapt to new procedures and practices.

Monitor the progress of the implementation regularly, tracking key milestones and addressing any challenges that arise. This may involve adjusting the action plan as needed to ensure that the improvements are effectively integrated into the organization's HR practices.

By diligently executing the action plan and providing the necessary resources and support, organizations can successfully implement the recommended improvements, leading to enhanced HR functions and overall organizational success.

- **Monitor Progress:** Monitoring progress is a critical step in ensuring that the implementation of HR audit recommendations is effective and yielding the desired results. This involves continuously tracking the progress of the action plan and measuring the impact of the changes using key performance indicators (KPIs).

  First, establish relevant KPIs that align with the goals of the audit recommendations. These could include metrics such as employee satisfaction, retention rates, training effectiveness, time-to-hire, and compliance rates. By defining these KPIs, organizations can quantitatively measure the success of the implemented changes.

  Next, set up regular monitoring and reporting processes to track these KPIs. This could involve monthly or quarterly reviews, progress reports, and meetings with key stakeholders. Regular monitoring helps identify any issues or roadblocks early on, allowing for timely adjustments to the action plan.

  Additionally, gather feedback from employees and managers to gain qualitative insights into the impact of the changes. Surveys, focus groups, and one-on-one interviews can provide valuable perspectives on how the new HR practices are perceived and experienced.

  By continuously monitoring progress and tracking KPIs, organizations can ensure that the implementation of audit recommendations is on track and driving the desired improvements. This proactive approach supports continuous improvement and helps create a more effective and responsive HR function.

- **Conduct Follow-Up Audits:** Conducting follow-up audits is essential for evaluating the effectiveness of the implemented changes and ensuring that the improvements are sustained over time. This process involves re-examining the areas previously audited to determine if the recommendations have been successfully implemented and if they have achieved the desired outcomes.

  During follow-up audits, auditors assess whether the action plan has been executed as intended and measure the impact of the changes using key performance indicators (KPIs). This helps identify any areas where the improvements may not be fully effective or where additional adjustments are needed.

  By regularly performing follow-up audits, organizations can maintain a continuous improvement cycle, ensuring that HR practices remain effective and aligned with organizational goals. If the follow-up findings reveal any gaps or ongoing issues, the action plan can be adjusted accordingly to address these challenges and further enhance HR functions.

  Overall, follow-up audits provide valuable feedback on the success of the implemented changes and help organizations sustain long-term improvements in their HR practices, ultimately contributing to a more efficient and productive work environment.

Key Areas to be Audited

- **HR Policies and Procedures:** Evaluating the organization's HR policies and procedures is a critical aspect of the HR audit process. This evaluation involves a comprehensive review of existing policies to ensure they are clear, consistent, compliant with legal requirements, and aligned with organizational goals.

  First, assess the clarity of HR policies and procedures. Policies should be written in plain language, easily understood by all employees. Clear policies help prevent misunderstandings and ensure that employees know their rights, responsibilities, and the organization's expectations.

  Next, evaluate the consistency of policies and procedures across the organization. Consistency is essential to ensure that all employees are treated fairly and equitably. Inconsistent policies can lead to confusion, potential grievances, and a perception of favoritism.

Compliance is another critical aspect of the evaluation. HR policies must adhere to local, national, and international labor laws and employment regulations. This includes compliance with anti-discrimination laws, wage and hour laws, health and safety regulations, and employee rights. Non-compliance can result in legal risks, fines, and damage to the organization's reputation.

Finally, ensure that HR policies and procedures are aligned with organizational goals. HR practices should support the strategic objectives of the organization, such as attracting and retaining top talent, fostering a positive work culture, and enhancing employee performance. Policies should be designed to drive organizational success while promoting employee well-being and development.

By thoroughly evaluating HR policies and procedures for clarity, consistency, compliance, and alignment with organizational goals, organizations can create a more effective and supportive HR framework that contributes to overall success.

- **Recruitment and Selection:** Assessing the effectiveness of recruitment and selection processes is essential for ensuring that an organization attracts and hires the right talent. This evaluation involves several key components, including job analysis, sourcing, interviewing, and hiring practices. Job analysis ensures that job descriptions accurately reflect the responsibilities, qualifications, and skills required for each position. Effective sourcing methods, such as job boards, social media, employee referrals, and recruitment agencies, help reach a diverse and qualified pool of candidates. The interviewing process should be structured, fair, and consistent, with standardized questions that assess candidates' qualifications, skills, and cultural fit. Efficient hiring practices minimize delays and ensure that the best candidates are hired promptly. By thoroughly assessing these components, organizations can identify strengths and weaknesses in their recruitment and selection processes, leading to more effective talent acquisition and a stronger workforce.

- **Training and Development:** Reviewing training and development programs is essential to ensure they align with both employee needs and organizational goals. This involves a thorough evaluation of the programs' content, delivery methods, and overall effectiveness.

First, assess whether the training programs address the skills and competencies required for employees to perform their roles effectively. This includes both technical skills and soft skills such as communication, leadership, and teamwork. Ensuring that training is relevant and up-to-date with industry standards and technological advancements is crucial.

Next, evaluate the delivery methods of the training programs. This could include in-person workshops, online courses, on-the-job training, or a combination of these. Assess the accessibility and convenience of the training for employees, as well as the effectiveness of each delivery method in engaging participants and facilitating learning.

Additionally, measure the impact of training programs on employee performance. This can be done through performance appraisals, feedback surveys, and analyzing key performance indicators (KPIs) such as productivity, quality of work, and employee retention rates. Identifying any improvements or gaps in performance helps determine the effectiveness of the training initiatives.

Finally, ensure that the training and development programs support the organization's strategic goals. This includes aligning training initiatives with business objectives, such as improving innovation, enhancing customer service, or preparing employees for leadership roles. By continuously reviewing and refining training programs, organizations can enhance employee skills, boost performance, and drive overall success.

- **Performance Management:** Evaluating an organization's performance management system involves a thorough assessment of several key components to ensure they effectively support employee growth and align with organizational goals. This includes examining the goal-setting process to verify that goals are specific, measurable, achievable, relevant, and time-bound (SMART), and that they are clearly communicated to employees. The performance appraisal process should be reviewed for fairness, transparency, and consistency, ensuring that criteria are well-defined and appraisals are conducted regularly. Additionally, the quality and frequency of feedback provided to employees should be evaluated, focusing on whether feedback is constructive, actionable, and supportive. Finally, the effectiveness of individual development plans (IDPs) should be assessed, ensuring they are tailored to each employee's needs and regularly updated to reflect progress and changing organizational priorities. This comprehensive evaluation helps identify strengths and weaknesses in the performance management system, leading to more effective employee development and alignment with organizational objectives.

- **Compensation and Benefits:** Assessing the competitiveness and fairness of an organization's compensation and benefits packages is crucial to attract and retain top talent. This evaluation involves a comprehensive review of the pay structures to ensure they are aligned with industry standards and commensurate with the roles and responsibilities of employees. It also includes analyzing incentive programs to determine their effectiveness in motivating and rewarding employees for their performance and contributions. Additionally, a thorough review of benefits offerings, such as health insurance, retirement plans, and paid leave, helps ensure they meet the needs and expectations of employees while remaining competitive in the job market. By evaluating these elements, organizations can ensure their compensation and benefits packages are fair, competitive, and supportive of employee well-being and satisfaction.

- **Employee Relations:** Reviewing employee relations practices is crucial for maintaining a harmonious and productive work environment. This assessment includes evaluating the organization's grievance handling procedures to ensure that employee concerns are addressed promptly and fairly. It also involves examining conflict resolution methods to determine their effectiveness in managing disputes and maintaining workplace harmony. Additionally, assessing the communication channels within the organization, both formal and informal, helps ensure that information flows smoothly and transparently, keeping employees informed and engaged. By thoroughly reviewing these areas, organizations can identify strengths and weaknesses in their employee relations practices, leading to improved grievance handling, effective conflict resolution, and enhanced communication, ultimately fostering a positive work culture.

- **HR Information Systems (HRIS):** Evaluating the effectiveness of HR Information Systems (HRIS) is crucial for managing and processing HR data efficiently. This assessment involves ensuring data accuracy, which is vital for informed decision-making and compliance. Regular audits help verify that employee records, payroll information, and other HR metrics are accurate and up-to-date. Accessibility is another key factor, as the HRIS should provide user-friendly interfaces that allow HR professionals, managers, and employees to quickly and efficiently access relevant information. Self-service options for employees to update their information or access documents are also important. Lastly, security measures must be thoroughly reviewed to protect HR data from unauthorized access, breaches, and cyber threats. This includes evaluating encryption protocols, access controls, and data backup procedures. By addressing these aspects, organizations can ensure their HRIS effectively supports data management, operational efficiency, and data security.

- **Compliance and Legal Issues:** Assessing compliance and legal issues in HR practices is vital for ensuring that the organization adheres to labor laws, employment regulations, and industry standards, while minimizing potential legal risks. This evaluation involves a comprehensive review of HR policies and procedures to ensure they are aligned with relevant legal requirements.

First, examine compliance with local, national, and international labor laws, such as wage and hour regulations, anti-discrimination laws, health and safety standards, and employee rights. This includes ensuring that hiring practices, compensation structures, workplace accommodations, and termination procedures meet legal standards. Regularly updating HR policies to reflect changes in legislation is crucial for maintaining compliance.

Next, assess adherence to industry-specific standards and best practices. This involves comparing the organization's HR practices with those of similar organizations to identify any discrepancies or areas for improvement. Benchmarking against industry standards helps ensure that the organization remains competitive and up-to-date with evolving HR trends.

Best Practices for the HR Audit Process

- **Involve Key Stakeholders:** Engaging key stakeholders in the HR audit process is crucial to ensure buy-in and support for the findings and recommendations. This involves actively involving HR leadership, managers, and employees at various stages of the audit to create a sense of ownership and collaboration.

First, involve HR leadership in defining the scope and objectives of the audit. Their insights and strategic perspective help align the audit with organizational goals. Keeping HR leadership informed about the audit's progress and preliminary findings ensures their continued support and engagement.

Next, engage managers by involving them in data collection and analysis. Managers possess valuable firsthand knowledge of HR practices and employee experiences. Their input helps provide a comprehensive understanding of the current state of HR functions. Additionally, involving managers in discussions about potential improvements fosters a sense of responsibility and accountability for implementing changes.

Include employees in the audit process through surveys, focus groups, and interviews. Gathering feedback from employees provides essential insights into their experiences, satisfaction levels, and areas for improvement. Involving employees in this way demonstrates that their opinions are valued and considered in decision-making.

Throughout the audit process, maintain open and transparent communication with all stakeholders. Regular updates, meetings, and feedback sessions help build trust and ensure everyone is aligned with the audit's objectives and outcomes.

By actively involving key stakeholders in the HR audit process, organizations can foster a collaborative environment, ensuring that the findings and recommendations are well-received and effectively implemented. This collaborative approach enhances the overall success of the HR audit and supports continuous improvement.

- **Maintain Objectivity:** Maintaining objectivity in an HR audit is crucial to ensure that the findings and recommendations are impartial and unbiased. To achieve this, it is important that the audit team is independent, with no conflicts of interest. This independence allows auditors to conduct a thorough and honest assessment without any undue influence or pressure.

  One effective way to ensure objectivity is to consider using external auditors or consultants. External auditors bring a fresh perspective and are not influenced by internal dynamics or relationships within the organization. Their impartiality helps provide a more accurate and credible assessment of HR practices.

  Additionally, having a diverse audit team with varied expertise and backgrounds can enhance objectivity. This diversity allows for multiple viewpoints and reduces the risk of biased interpretations or conclusions.

  Implementing strict confidentiality protocols is also essential to protect the integrity of the audit process. Auditors should have access to all necessary information while ensuring that sensitive data is handled with care and confidentiality.

By maintaining objectivity and using external auditors or consultants, organizations can ensure that their HR audits are impartial and provide valuable insights for improving HR practices and achieving organizational goals.

- **Use Multiple Data Sources:** To obtain a comprehensive view of HR practices, it's essential to collect data from multiple sources, such as documents, surveys, interviews, and observations. Document reviews provide a baseline understanding of formal HR policies and procedures, while surveys gather quantitative feedback from employees on various aspects of HR, such as job satisfaction and training effectiveness. Interviews offer qualitative insights through in-depth discussions with employees, managers, and HR professionals, uncovering issues not evident in surveys. Observations of HR processes in action, like recruitment activities and performance appraisals, provide real-time insights into the implementation of practices. By using these diverse data sources, organizations can triangulate findings, ensuring a thorough and accurate assessment of HR practices, leading to more effective HR strategies and initiatives.

- **Focus on Continuous Improvement:** Focusing on continuous improvement is key to maximizing the benefits of the HR audit process. Rather than viewing the audit as a one-time assessment, it should be seen as an ongoing opportunity to enhance HR practices. Implementing regular audits allows organizations to monitor progress, identify new areas for improvement, and adapt to changing circumstances and regulations. By regularly revisiting HR practices and policies, organizations can ensure they remain effective, compliant, and aligned with strategic goals. Continuous audits also foster a culture of accountability and proactive problem-solving, leading to ongoing enhancements in HR functions and overall organizational performance. This approach promotes sustained growth and improvement, contributing to long-term success.

- **Communicate Transparently:** Communicating transparently during the HR audit process is vital for building trust and ensuring that all relevant stakeholders understand the purpose, scope, and findings of the audit. Start by clearly articulating the audit's objectives, the areas it will cover, and the methodologies used. This initial communication helps set expectations and fosters an open environment.

Once the audit is complete, share the key findings and recommendations in a straightforward manner. Use clear and concise language, supported by data visualizations if necessary, to make the information accessible and understandable to all stakeholders. It's important to highlight both strengths and areas for improvement, ensuring a balanced and honest assessment.

Providing regular updates on the progress of implementing recommended improvements is equally important. This can be done through periodic reports, meetings, and presentations. Keeping stakeholders informed about the steps being taken, the challenges encountered, and the milestones achieved helps maintain momentum and demonstrates the organization's commitment to continuous improvement.

By communicating transparently, organizations can foster a culture of accountability and collaboration, ensuring that the audit process is seen as a positive and constructive endeavor aimed at enhancing HR practices and overall organizational performance.

- **Infosys Limited:** Infosys conducts regular HR audits to ensure compliance, identify areas for improvement, and align HR practices with organizational goals. The company's commitment to continuous improvement has resulted in enhanced HR efficiency and employee satisfaction.
- **Tata Consultancy Services (TCS):** TCS uses HR audits to benchmark its HR practices against industry standards and identify best practices. The company's focus on data-driven audits has led to improved HR performance and strategic alignment.

Conclusion

The HR Audit process is a valuable tool for evaluating and improving an organization's HR policies, practices, and systems. By conducting regular audits, organizations can ensure compliance, enhance performance, and align HR practices with strategic goals. Despite challenges, the benefits of a well-executed HR audit make it an essential practice for modern organizations committed to optimizing their workforce and achieving sustainable growth.

BENEFITS OF HR AUDIT

Introduction to the Benefits of Human Resource Audit

A Human Resource (HR) Audit is a systematic and comprehensive evaluation of an organization's HR policies, practices, systems, and procedures. Conducting regular HR audits provides several benefits that contribute to the overall success and sustainability of an organization. This chapter explores the key benefits of HR audits and how they enhance organizational performance.

Key Benefits of Human Resource Audit

Compliance and Risk Management

- **Ensuring Compliance:** Human Resources (HR) audits play a crucial role in ensuring that an organization's HR practices are in full compliance with legal and regulatory requirements. By conducting comprehensive evaluations of HR policies, procedures, and documentation, organizations can identify potential compliance issues and rectify them proactively. These audits cover various aspects such as employment law, wage and hour regulations, benefits administration, and workplace safety standards.

  The primary goal of HR audits is to reduce the risk of legal issues, penalties, and fines that could arise from non-compliance. By regularly reviewing and updating HR practices, organizations can ensure they meet all relevant laws and regulations, thereby safeguarding themselves against potential legal challenges. Additionally, HR audits provide an opportunity to streamline HR processes, improve efficiency, and enhance overall organizational governance.

  By maintaining compliance through HR audits, organizations not only protect themselves legally but also foster a positive work environment that upholds ethical standards and employee rights. This proactive approach contributes to long-term organizational success and stability.

- **Identifying Risks:** HR audits are essential for identifying potential legal and regulatory risks associated with HR practices. By systematically reviewing and analyzing HR policies, procedures, and documentation, audits uncover areas of non-compliance, such as violations of employment laws, inadequate wage and hour practices, and insufficient benefits administration. This detailed examination enables organizations to take corrective actions, such as updating policies, retraining staff, and implementing new compliance measures. By addressing these risks proactively, organizations can mitigate the likelihood of legal disputes, penalties, and fines, ensuring a more secure and legally compliant HR environment. Regular HR audits contribute to continuous improvement and help maintain a positive reputation and trust among employees and stakeholders.

Performance Improvement

- **Identifying Strengths and Weaknesses:** HR audits play a crucial role in evaluating the effectiveness of an organization's HR policies and practices. By systematically reviewing HR processes, documentation, and compliance, audits help identify both strengths and areas for improvement. This comprehensive assessment provides valuable insights into what is working well and where there may be gaps or inefficiencies.

  Identifying strengths allows organizations to build on successful practices, ensuring that they continue to support employee satisfaction, engagement, and productivity. On the other hand, recognizing weaknesses enables organizations to take targeted corrective actions, such as updating policies, improving training programs, or enhancing communication strategies.

  Overall, HR audits contribute to the continuous improvement of the HR function, leading to better resource allocation, increased compliance, and ultimately, enhanced organizational performance.

- **Optimizing Processes:** HR audits are instrumental in optimizing HR processes by uncovering inefficiencies and redundancies. By systematically examining various aspects of HR operations, audits highlight areas where processes may be duplicated, outdated, or unnecessarily complex. This detailed analysis enables organizations to identify opportunities for streamlining workflows, eliminating unnecessary steps, and adopting more efficient practices.

For instance, an audit may reveal that multiple departments are performing similar tasks independently, leading to duplicated efforts and wasted resources. By consolidating these tasks and establishing a more coordinated approach, organizations can reduce redundancy and improve overall efficiency. Similarly, audits may identify outdated manual processes that can be automated, freeing up HR personnel to focus on more strategic activities.

The insights gained from HR audits help organizations implement targeted improvements that enhance operational efficiency, reduce costs, and improve the overall effectiveness of the HR function. By continuously optimizing HR processes, organizations can create a more agile and responsive HR department that better supports the organization's strategic goals.

Strategic Alignment

- **Aligning HR with Organizational Goals:** HR audits are vital in ensuring that HR practices align with the organization's strategic goals and objectives. By systematically evaluating HR policies, procedures, and initiatives, audits help identify whether they are supporting or hindering the achievement of these goals. This alignment is crucial for maximizing the HR function's contribution to overall organizational success.

  When HR practices are in harmony with strategic objectives, the HR function can more effectively support talent management, employee engagement, and workforce planning. For instance, if an organization's goal is to foster innovation, HR audits can ensure that recruitment, training, and development programs are designed to attract and nurture creative talent. Similarly, if a company's objective is to enhance customer service, HR audits can verify that performance management systems emphasize customer-centric behaviors and skills.

  Aligning HR practices with organizational goals also facilitates better resource allocation, as HR investments are directed toward initiatives that directly contribute to strategic outcomes. This targeted approach enhances the efficiency and impact of HR efforts, ultimately driving the organization's overall performance and competitiveness. By continuously monitoring and adjusting HR practices through regular audits, organizations can ensure sustained alignment with their evolving strategic goals.

- **Supporting Strategic Decision-Making:** HR audits are instrumental in supporting strategic decision-making by providing valuable data and insights into various HR functions. By systematically evaluating HR policies, procedures, and practices, audits help organizations identify strengths, weaknesses, and areas for improvement. This comprehensive analysis equips HR leaders and management with the information needed to make informed decisions regarding talent management, workforce planning, and resource allocation.

  In talent management, HR audits reveal gaps in skills, performance, and employee engagement, enabling organizations to develop targeted strategies for recruitment, training, and retention. For workforce planning, audits provide insights into demographic trends, turnover rates, and future staffing needs, allowing organizations to proactively address potential shortages and optimize workforce composition. In terms of resource allocation, audits highlight inefficiencies and redundancies, enabling organizations to streamline processes and allocate resources more effectively.

  Overall, the data and insights gained from HR audits empower organizations to make strategic decisions that align with their business goals, enhance operational efficiency, and drive long-term success. By leveraging audit findings, organizations can continuously improve their HR practices and ensure they are well-positioned to meet evolving challenges and opportunities.

Employee Engagement and Satisfaction

- **Enhancing Employee Experience:** HR audits play a pivotal role in enhancing the employee experience by assessing engagement and satisfaction levels within the organization. Through comprehensive surveys, interviews, and data analysis, HR audits gather valuable insights into employees' perceptions and experiences. This information helps identify areas where improvements can be made, such as communication, work-life balance, career development, and recognition programs.

By addressing these areas, organizations can create a more supportive and motivating work environment, which in turn fosters higher levels of job satisfaction and engagement. For example, if an audit reveals that employees feel undervalued, the organization can implement more robust recognition and reward systems. Similarly, if work-life balance is a concern, flexible working arrangements and wellness programs can be introduced.

Ultimately, HR audits help organizations to continuously refine their HR practices, ensuring that they align with employees' needs and expectations. This proactive approach leads to a more positive work environment, where employees feel valued, supported, and motivated to contribute to the organization's success.

- **Promoting Fairness and Transparency:** HR audits play a crucial role in promoting fairness and transparency within organizations. By thoroughly evaluating and improving HR policies and practices, audits help ensure that all employees are treated equitably and that organizational processes are transparent. This involves assessing various HR functions, such as recruitment, compensation, performance management, and employee relations, to identify any potential biases, inconsistencies, or areas of non-compliance.

By addressing these issues, organizations can implement more consistent and fair HR practices that build trust and credibility among employees. For instance, an audit may reveal disparities in pay or promotion opportunities, prompting the organization to take corrective actions and establish more equitable policies. Similarly, by enhancing transparency in decision-making processes, organizations can foster a culture of openness and accountability.

Overall, HR audits contribute to creating a positive work environment where employees feel valued, respected, and confident that their concerns are heard and addressed. This, in turn, enhances employee satisfaction, engagement, and overall organizational performance.

Cost Management and Resource Optimization

- **Identifying Cost Savings:** HR audits are instrumental in identifying cost-saving opportunities within organizations. By meticulously examining HR practices, processes, and resource allocation, audits can pinpoint inefficiencies, redundancies, and unnecessary expenses. For instance, an audit might reveal duplicated efforts across different departments, outdated or manual processes that could be automated, and roles that no longer align with the organization's strategic goals.

By addressing these inefficiencies, organizations can streamline their operations, eliminate redundant roles, and reduce unnecessary expenditures. This not only optimizes resource utilization but also enhances overall operational efficiency. The cost savings realized through these improvements can be significant, allowing organizations to reinvest in strategic initiatives, employee development, or technology upgrades.

Ultimately, HR audits help organizations achieve a leaner and more effective HR function, contributing to better financial performance and a stronger competitive position in the market.

- **Efficient Resource Allocation:** HR audits provide valuable insights into an organization's workforce needs and resource allocation by systematically evaluating HR processes, employee performance, and resource utilization. Through this comprehensive assessment, audits can identify areas where resources may be underutilized or misallocated, allowing organizations to make informed decisions about optimizing their workforce.

For example, an audit might reveal that certain departments are overstaffed while others face critical skill shortages. By reallocating resources to address these imbalances, organizations can ensure that they have the right talent in the right roles to meet business demands. Additionally, audits can uncover opportunities to streamline HR processes, such as automating manual tasks or consolidating redundant roles, further enhancing efficiency.

By providing a clear understanding of workforce needs and resource utilization, HR audits enable organizations to allocate resources more effectively and efficiently. This targeted approach not only improves operational performance but also supports strategic goals by ensuring that HR investments are aligned with the organization's priorities. Ultimately, efficient resource allocation leads to cost savings, increased productivity, and a stronger competitive position in the market.

Benchmarking and Best Practices

- **Benchmarking Against Industry Standards:** HR audits play a vital role in benchmarking an organization's HR practices against industry standards and best practices. By conducting thorough evaluations, organizations can compare their policies, procedures, and performance metrics with those of leading companies in the industry. This benchmarking process helps identify gaps and areas where the organization may be falling short of best practices.

  For instance, an HR audit might reveal that an organization's employee engagement initiatives are less effective than those of industry leaders. This insight enables the organization to implement new strategies or improve existing ones to enhance employee satisfaction and productivity. Additionally, benchmarking against industry standards ensures that the organization remains competitive and compliant with evolving regulations and expectations.

  Overall, HR audits provide a clear roadmap for continuous improvement by highlighting strengths and pinpointing areas for development. By adopting best practices from the industry, organizations can optimize their HR functions, leading to better talent management, increased operational efficiency, and enhanced overall performance.

- **Adopting Best Practices:** HR audits are instrumental in uncovering best practices in HR management, which organizations can then adopt to enhance their HR functions. By systematically evaluating current HR policies, procedures, and practices, audits can identify successful strategies and processes used by leading organizations within the industry.

  For instance, an audit may reveal effective recruitment and onboarding practices that significantly reduce time-to-hire and improve employee retention. It may also highlight innovative approaches to performance management, such as continuous feedback systems that foster a culture of ongoing development and accountability. Additionally, audits can identify comprehensive employee engagement programs that effectively boost morale and productivity.

  By adopting these best practices, organizations can improve their HR functions, making them more efficient and aligned with industry standards. This not only enhances the overall employee experience but also contributes to achieving strategic organizational goals. Implementing best practices helps ensure that the HR function remains competitive, proactive, and capable of supporting the organization's growth and success.

Continuous Improvement

- **Driving Continuous Improvement:** HR audits play a crucial role in fostering a culture of continuous improvement within organizations. By regularly evaluating and enhancing HR practices, audits help organizations stay competitive and adaptable in a constantly changing business environment. This ongoing process involves assessing current HR policies, identifying areas for improvement, and implementing best practices to address any gaps or inefficiencies.

  Through continuous monitoring and evaluation, HR audits ensure that HR functions remain aligned with organizational goals and industry standards. This proactive approach helps organizations anticipate and respond to emerging challenges and opportunities, ultimately driving overall performance and success. By committing to regular HR audits, organizations can create a dynamic and responsive HR function that supports sustainable growth and long-term competitiveness.

- **Encouraging Innovation:** HR audits play a pivotal role in encouraging innovation within organizations by prompting HR professionals to explore creative solutions and improvements. During the audit process, areas of inefficiency and gaps in HR practices are identified, which acts as a catalyst for thinking outside the box and developing innovative strategies to address these challenges. This could include adopting new technologies, implementing modern HR practices, or redesigning workflows to enhance efficiency and effectiveness.

  Furthermore, by regularly conducting HR audits, organizations create a culture of continuous improvement, where innovation is not just encouraged but expected. HR professionals are inspired to stay current with industry trends, experiment with new ideas, and continuously seek ways to improve the employee experience and organizational performance. This ongoing commitment to innovation helps organizations stay competitive, adapt to changing business environments, and drive long-term success.

Enhancing Organizational Culture

- **Fostering a Positive Work Environment:** HR audits are instrumental in fostering a positive work environment by assessing the organization's culture and identifying areas for improvement. Through comprehensive evaluations, audits provide insights into employee well-being, engagement, and collaboration. By examining factors such as communication practices, leadership effectiveness, and workplace inclusivity, HR audits reveal opportunities to enhance the overall employee experience.

  For instance, an audit might uncover issues with communication channels, leading to the implementation of more effective communication strategies that promote transparency and trust. Similarly, audits may identify gaps in employee engagement initiatives, prompting the development of programs that boost morale and job satisfaction. By addressing these areas, organizations can create a more supportive and collaborative work environment.

  Overall, HR audits play a crucial role in enhancing organizational culture, ensuring that employees feel valued, engaged, and motivated. This not only improves employee well-being but also drives higher productivity and overall organizational success.

- **Promoting Diversity and Inclusion:** HR audits play a crucial role in promoting diversity and inclusion within organizations. By thoroughly evaluating HR practices related to recruitment, hiring, training, and promotions, audits can identify any biases, gaps, or barriers that may exist. This evaluation process helps organizations develop and implement strategies to foster a more inclusive and equitable work environment.

  For example, audits can reveal disparities in hiring practices, such as a lack of diversity in applicant pools or biased interview processes. By addressing these issues, organizations can implement fairer recruitment practices, ensuring that all candidates have equal opportunities. Additionally, audits can assess the effectiveness of diversity training programs, ensuring they are impactful and aligned with the organization's goals.

  Furthermore, HR audits can uncover disparities in career advancement opportunities, highlighting the need for mentorship programs or targeted development initiatives to support underrepresented groups. By taking proactive steps to address these issues, organizations can create a more inclusive culture where all employees feel valued and respected.

Overall, by promoting diversity and inclusion through regular HR audits, organizations can build a more equitable workplace that supports the success and well-being of all employees.

Conclusion

Conducting regular Human Resource Audits provides numerous benefits that contribute to the overall success and sustainability of an organization. From ensuring compliance and risk management to enhancing employee engagement and promoting continuous improvement, HR audits play a crucial role in optimizing the HR function and aligning it with organizational goals. Despite challenges, the benefits of a well-executed HR audit make it an essential practice for modern organizations committed to achieving excellence and sustainable growth.

CHAPTER TWENTY-FIVE

Case Studies and Practical Examples

Introduction to Case Studies and Practical Examples

Case studies and practical examples provide valuable insights into the real-world application of Human Resource Accounting (HRA) and its impact on organizational performance. By examining how different organizations implement HRA practices, we can learn about the benefits, challenges, and best practices associated with this field. This chapter presents a series of case studies and practical examples from various organizations that have successfully implemented HRA.

Case Study 1: Infosys Limited

Background: Infosys Limited is a global leader in consulting, technology, and outsourcing solutions. With a strong focus on human capital, Infosys has been a pioneer in integrating HRA into its financial reporting and strategic planning processes.

HRA Practices:

- **Present Value of Future Earnings:** Infosys uses the present value of future earnings method to quantify the economic value of its human resources. This approach involves projecting the future earnings of employees and discounting them to present value.

- **Training and Development Investment:** Infosys invests significantly in employee training and development through its Global Education Center. The company quantifies the costs associated with training programs and measures the ROI of these investments.

Outcomes:

Enhanced Financial Reporting: By incorporating the value of human resources into its financial statements, Infosys provides stakeholders with a comprehensive view of its assets and performance.

Increased Employee Retention: The company's focus on employee development has led to higher retention rates and a more engaged workforce.

Strategic Decision-Making: HRA data supports strategic HR decisions, such as workforce planning, talent management, and resource allocation.

Case Study 2: Tata Consultancy Services (TCS)

Background: Tata Consultancy Services (TCS) is a leading IT services, consulting, and business solutions organization. TCS has been at the forefront of adopting HRA practices to enhance its HR function and overall organizational performance.

HRA Practices:

- **Replacement Cost Method:** TCS uses the replacement cost method to estimate the cost of replacing employees with similar skills and experience. This method helps the company understand the financial impact of employee turnover.
- **Human Resource Valuation through Mergers and Acquisitions:** During mergers and acquisitions, TCS evaluates the market value of the acquired workforce to determine the overall worth of the acquisition.

Outcomes:

Improved Cost Management: By understanding the costs associated with employee turnover, TCS can implement effective retention strategies and reduce turnover-related expenses.

- **Informed M&A Decisions:** The valuation of human resources during mergers and acquisitions ensures that TCS makes informed decisions and achieves successful integrations.
- **Strategic Alignment:** HRA data aligns HR practices with organizational goals, supporting strategic planning and performance improvement.

Case Study 3: Google

Background: Google is a global technology company known for its innovative products and services. Google's strong emphasis on human capital has driven the company's success and growth.

HRA Practices:

- **Human Capital Measurement:** Google measures the value of its human capital by assessing employee skills, knowledge, and performance. The company uses a combination of quantitative and qualitative methods to capture the economic value of its workforce.
- **Employee Well-being and Development:** Google invests in employee well-being and development through comprehensive benefits, wellness programs, and continuous learning opportunities.

Outcomes:

- **High Employee Engagement:** Google's focus on employee well-being and development has led to high levels of engagement and job satisfaction.
- **Innovation and Productivity:** The company's emphasis on human capital has driven innovation and productivity, contributing to its market leadership.
- **Attraction and Retention of Top Talent:** Google's reputation as an employer of choice attracts top talent from around the world, ensuring a continuous influx of skilled employees.
- **Practical Example:** Implementing HRA in a Mid-Sized Organization
- **Background:** A mid-sized manufacturing company with 500 employees seeks to implement HRA practices to enhance its HR function and overall performance.

HRA Practices:

Data Collection: The company implements an HR information system (HRIS) to collect and manage data on employee performance, skills, training, and compensation.

Valuation Method: The company uses the present value of future earnings method to quantify the economic value of its human resources. This involves projecting future earnings based on performance data and discounting them to present value.

Training and Development Programs: The company invests in employee training and development to enhance skills and productivity. The costs associated with these programs are measured and evaluated for ROI.

Outcomes:

- **Enhanced Financial Reporting:** The inclusion of human resource values in financial statements provides stakeholders with a comprehensive view of the company's assets and performance.
- **Improved Decision-Making:** HRA data supports informed decision-making related to talent management, workforce planning, and resource allocation.
- **Increased Employee Engagement:** The company's focus on employee development and well-being leads to higher levels of engagement and job satisfaction.

Conclusion

Case studies and practical examples demonstrate the real-world application of Human Resource Accounting and its impact on organizational performance. By examining the experiences of different organizations, we can learn valuable lessons about the benefits, challenges, and best practices associated with HRA. These insights can guide other organizations in successfully implementing HRA practices and achieving sustainable growth.

CHAPTER TWENTY-SIX

Successful Implementation in Organizations

Introduction to Successful Implementation

Implementing Human Resource Accounting (HRA) successfully requires careful planning, execution, and continuous improvement. Organizations that effectively integrate HRA practices into their operations can achieve enhanced decision-making, strategic alignment, and overall performance. This chapter outlines the key steps and best practices for successfully implementing HRA in organizations, illustrated with practical examples.

Key Steps for Successful Implementation

Gain Leadership Support

- **Description:** Strong support from organizational leadership is crucial for the successful implementation of HRA. Leaders play a vital role in championing HRA initiatives, allocating resources, and fostering a culture that values human capital.
- **Example:** Infosys Limited's leadership actively supports HRA practices by integrating them into the company's strategic goals and ensuring that necessary resources are allocated for data collection and analysis.

Conduct a Pilot Program

- **Description:** Implementing a pilot program allows organizations to test HRA practices on a smaller scale before full-scale deployment. This helps identify potential issues, gather feedback, and make necessary adjustments.
- **Example:** Tata Consultancy Services (TCS) conducted pilot programs to test the present value of future earnings method for quantifying human resources. The insights gained from the pilot helped refine the methodology for broader implementation.

Develop a Comprehensive HRA Framework

- **Description:** Create a detailed HRA framework that outlines the methods, metrics, and processes for measuring and reporting the value of human resources. Ensure that the framework aligns with organizational goals and industry standards.
- **Example:** Google developed a comprehensive HRA framework that combines quantitative and qualitative methods to assess the value of its human capital. This framework supports strategic decision-making and aligns with the company's focus on innovation and employee well-being.

Leverage Technology and Data Analytics

- **Description:** Use technology and data analytics tools to enhance data collection, analysis, and reporting. HR information systems (HRIS) and analytics platforms can improve the accuracy and efficiency of HRA practices.
- **Example:** A mid-sized manufacturing company implemented an HRIS to collect and manage data on employee performance, skills, and compensation. This technology-driven approach streamlined data collection and supported accurate HRA analysis.

Ensure Data Privacy and Confidentiality

- **Description:** Establish clear policies and procedures for data privacy and confidentiality to protect employee information. Ensure compliance with data protection regulations and obtain informed consent from employees.

- **Example:** Infosys Limited ensures data privacy and confidentiality by implementing robust data security measures and adhering to data protection regulations. The company obtains informed consent from employees for data collection and analysis.

Engage Stakeholders and Communicate Transparently

- **Description:** Involve key stakeholders, including HR professionals, managers, and employees, in the development and implementation of HRA practices. Communicate the objectives, benefits, and processes of HRA transparently to build trust and support.
- **Example:** TCS engages stakeholders by involving cross-functional teams in the HRA implementation process. The company communicates the purpose and benefits of HRA to employees and managers, fostering a collaborative approach.

Monitor and Evaluate Progress

- **Description:** Continuously monitor and evaluate the progress of HRA implementation. Use key performance indicators (KPIs) to measure the impact of HRA practices and identify areas for improvement.
- **Example:** Google regularly monitors the impact of its HRA practices through KPIs such as employee engagement, retention rates, and performance metrics. The company uses this data to make informed adjustments and drive continuous improvement.

Best Practices for Successful Implementation

- **Align with Organizational Goals:** Ensure that HRA practices align with the organization's strategic goals and objectives. This alignment enhances the relevance and impact of HRA on overall performance.
- **Standardize Methods and Metrics:** Develop standardized methods and metrics for measuring and reporting the value of human resources. This ensures consistency and comparability in HRA practices.
- **Promote a Culture of Continuous Improvement:** Foster a culture that values continuous improvement and innovation. Regularly review and update HRA practices to reflect changes in the workforce and market conditions.

- **Provide Training and Support:** Offer training and support to HR professionals and managers to ensure they understand and effectively implement HRA practices. Continuous learning and development are essential for successful HRA implementation.
- **Focus on Transparency and Fairness:** Ensure that HRA practices are transparent and fair. Communicate the criteria and processes used for measuring and valuing human resources to build trust and credibility.

Case Studies and Practical Examples

- **Infosys Limited:** Infosys successfully implemented HRA by securing leadership support, conducting training programs, and leveraging technology for data collection and analysis. The company's integrated reporting system combines HRA data with financial data, providing comprehensive insights.
- **Tata Consultancy Services (TCS):** TCS overcame implementation challenges by forming cross-functional teams and using pilot programs to test HRA practices. The company's commitment to data privacy and transparency has built trust among employees and stakeholders.
- **Google:** Google's comprehensive HRA framework combines quantitative and qualitative methods to assess the value of its human capital. The company's focus on employee well-being and development drives innovation and productivity, contributing to its market leadership.

Conclusion

Successfully implementing Human Resource Accounting requires careful planning, execution, and continuous improvement. By gaining leadership support, conducting pilot programs, developing a comprehensive HRA framework, leveraging technology, ensuring data privacy, engaging stakeholders, and monitoring progress, organizations can achieve enhanced decision-making, strategic alignment, and overall performance. The experiences of organizations like Infosys, TCS, and Google provide valuable lessons and best practices for successfully implementing HRA and realizing its benefits.

CHAPTER TWENTY-SEVEN

COMPARATIVE ANALYSIS

Introduction to Comparative Analysis

Comparative analysis in Human Resource Accounting (HRA) involves evaluating and contrasting HRA practices across different organizations, industries, and geographical regions. By comparing HRA methodologies, outcomes, and best practices, organizations can identify trends, benchmark their performance, and adopt strategies to enhance their HRA practices. This chapter explores the key aspects of comparative analysis in HRA and provides insights into how organizations can benefit from such evaluations.

Key Aspects of Comparative Analysis

Methodologies and Approaches

- **Cost-Based Methods:** Compare how organizations use cost-based methods, such as historical cost, replacement cost, and training and development cost, to measure the value of human resources. Analyze the effectiveness and challenges associated with each method.
- **Value-Based Methods:** Evaluate the adoption of value-based methods, such as the present value of future earnings, economic value added (EVA), and human asset multiplier, across different organizations. Assess the accuracy and reliability of these methods in quantifying human capital.

Integration with Financial Reporting

- **Financial Statements:** Organizations integrate Human Resource Accounting (HRA) data into their financial statements in various ways, reflecting the value of human capital alongside traditional financial metrics. This integration may include reporting on recruitment costs, training expenses, employee development, and the potential future economic benefits derived from human resources. By incorporating human resource values, organizations provide a more comprehensive view of their assets and liabilities, highlighting the strategic importance of human capital in achieving business objectives. The inclusion of HRA data can significantly impact stakeholder perceptions, as investors and analysts gain a clearer understanding of the organization's investment in its workforce and the potential return on these investments. This transparency fosters trust and confidence among stakeholders, demonstrating a commitment to valuing and developing employees. Additionally, it can influence stock prices, as the market recognizes the critical role of human capital in driving long-term growth and sustainability. Overall, integrating HRA data into financial statements offers a holistic view of an organization's value, promoting better decision-making and fostering a culture of accountability and transparency.

- **Transparency and Disclosure:** Evaluating the transparency and disclosure practices of organizations in reporting Human Resource Accounting (HRA) data reveals varying degrees of effectiveness. While some organizations have adopted comprehensive reporting practices that clearly communicate human resource values, others may still be opaque or inconsistent in their disclosures. Best practices for clear and comprehensive communication of human resource values to stakeholders include: prioritizing transparency in senior leadership communication about HR policies and culture, ensuring consistent and relevant messaging, promoting pay transparency to build trust and accountability, actively listening to employees and addressing their feedback, and providing confidential channels for employee input. By implementing these practices, organizations can foster trust, engage their workforce, and demonstrate their commitment to valuing human capital, ultimately enhancing stakeholder perceptions and organizational reputation.

Strategic Human Resource Management (HRM)

- **Alignment with Organizational Goals:** Organizations align their Human Resource Accounting (HRA) practices with strategic Human Resource Management (HRM) goals to ensure that HR initiatives support overall business objectives. By integrating HRA with strategic HRM, organizations can more effectively manage talent, plan their workforce, and allocate resources.

  In supporting talent management, HRA provides insights into employee performance, development needs, and career progression. This information helps organizations identify high-potential employees, design targeted training programs, and implement retention strategies that align with long-term business goals.

  For workforce planning, HRA data is used to forecast future workforce needs, identify skill gaps, and develop strategies to address these gaps. By analyzing historical data and trends, organizations can anticipate changes in the labor market and plan accordingly, ensuring they have the right talent in place to meet business demands.

  In terms of resource allocation, HRA helps organizations make informed decisions about where to invest in employee development, compensation, and benefits. By understanding the value and impact of their human capital, organizations can allocate resources more effectively, prioritizing initiatives that drive the greatest return on investment.

  Overall, the alignment of HRA practices with strategic HRM goals enhances the effectiveness of HR initiatives, supports organizational growth, and ensures that human capital is managed in a way that maximizes its value to the business.

- **Performance Management:** Human Resource Accounting (HRA) plays a crucial role in performance management systems by providing valuable data to set performance benchmarks, identify development opportunities, and reward employee contributions.

  Through HRA, organizations gather detailed information on employee performance, skills, and achievements. This data serves as the foundation for setting realistic and attainable performance benchmarks that align with organizational goals. By comparing individual performance against these benchmarks, organizations can objectively evaluate employee contributions and identify areas where improvement is needed.

HRA data also helps in identifying development opportunities for employees. By analyzing performance trends and skill gaps, organizations can design targeted training programs that address specific needs, ensuring employees have the necessary skills and knowledge to excel in their roles. This approach fosters continuous learning and growth, enhancing overall workforce capabilities.

Moreover, HRA data enables organizations to implement fair and transparent reward systems. By recognizing and rewarding employees based on objective performance metrics, organizations can motivate their workforce and encourage high levels of productivity. This approach not only boosts morale but also promotes a culture of excellence and accountability.

Overall, HRA enhances the effectiveness of performance management systems by providing data-driven insights that support informed decision-making, development planning, and recognition of employee contributions, ultimately driving organizational success.

Compliance and Risk Management

- **Legal Compliance:** Organizations ensure compliance with labor laws, employment regulations, and industry standards through meticulous Human Resource Accounting (HRA) practices. These practices involve maintaining detailed records of employee contracts, wages, working hours, and benefits, conducting regular audits, and providing training on legal requirements. HRA helps organizations stay proactive in identifying and addressing compliance issues, reducing the risk of legal violations. By benchmarking against industry standards and transparently reporting HR practices, organizations build trust with stakeholders and regulatory bodies. The effectiveness of HRA in mitigating legal and regulatory risks lies in its ability to provide accurate documentation and evidence, support proactive compliance measures, and enhance the organization's reputation for adhering to legal and ethical standards. Through these efforts, HRA ensures that organizations manage their human capital responsibly while safeguarding against potential legal challenges.

- **Risk Identification and Mitigation:** Organizations leverage Human Resource Accounting (HRA) data to identify and mitigate HR-related risks such as workforce shortages, skill gaps, and employee turnover.

By analyzing comprehensive HR data, organizations can forecast future staffing needs and address potential workforce shortages through targeted recruitment and succession planning. HRA data helps identify skill gaps within the workforce, enabling the design of tailored training programs to upskill employees and ensure they possess the necessary competencies. Additionally, HRA data provides insights into employee turnover patterns, allowing organizations to understand the root causes of turnover and implement effective retention strategies. By proactively managing these HR-related risks, organizations can maintain a stable, skilled, and satisfied workforce, ultimately enhancing overall organizational performance.

Employee Engagement and Retention

- **Employee Satisfaction:** The impact of Human Resource Accounting (HRA) practices on employee satisfaction and engagement varies across organizations. Effective HRA practices that transparently recognize and value employee contributions tend to result in higher levels of satisfaction and engagement. Organizations that prioritize transparent communication, fair recognition, professional development opportunities, work-life balance, and active employee feedback generally see more positive outcomes in employee morale and motivation. Best practices for using HRA to enhance the employee experience include regularly sharing HR policies and performance metrics, implementing equitable reward systems, offering targeted training programs, promoting flexible work arrangements, and creating channels for employee feedback. By adopting these practices, organizations can foster a supportive and motivating work environment, leading to increased employee satisfaction and engagement.

- **Retention Strategies:** Organizations leverage Human Resource Accounting (HRA) data to develop and implement effective retention strategies by analyzing employee performance, engagement, and turnover trends. By examining this data, organizations can identify patterns and factors contributing to employee attrition, such as job dissatisfaction, lack of career growth, or inadequate compensation.

  Retention strategies informed by HRA data often include targeted interventions such as career development programs, competitive compensation packages, and enhanced employee engagement initiatives.

By addressing the specific needs and concerns of employees, these strategies aim to improve job satisfaction and reduce turnover.

The success of these retention strategies is measured by tracking key metrics such as turnover rates, employee engagement scores, and retention of top talent. Organizations that effectively use HRA data to implement tailored retention strategies often see a significant reduction in turnover and higher levels of employee satisfaction and loyalty. This proactive approach not only helps retain top talent but also fosters a positive work environment, ultimately contributing to the organization's long-term success.

Cost Management and Efficiency

- **Resource Optimization:** Organizations use Human Resource Accounting (HRA) data to optimize resource allocation and improve cost management by analyzing employee productivity, resource utilization, and operational costs. By leveraging HRA data, organizations can identify areas where resources are underutilized or overextended, allowing them to make informed decisions about reallocating resources to maximize efficiency.

  For example, HRA data can reveal patterns in workforce performance, helping organizations identify high-performing employees and allocate them to critical projects or roles where their skills are most needed. Additionally, HRA data can highlight areas with excessive labor costs, prompting organizations to streamline processes or implement automation to reduce expenses.

  The impact of HRA on reducing inefficiencies and achieving cost savings is significant. Organizations that effectively use HRA data to optimize resource allocation often experience increased productivity, reduced labor costs, and enhanced operational efficiency. By minimizing waste and ensuring that resources are used effectively, these organizations can achieve substantial cost savings and improve their overall financial performance. This proactive approach to resource management also supports long-term sustainability and competitiveness in the market.

- **Investment in Employee Development:** Evaluating the ROI of investments in employee training and development across organizations reveals significant benefits, including increased productivity, higher employee engagement, and improved retention rates. Effective training programs lead to a more skilled and capable workforce, which directly contributes to organizational success. Best practices for measuring and maximizing returns include setting clear training objectives, identifying relevant metrics (such as productivity improvements and employee performance), conducting benchmark assessments, linking training initiatives to business goals, and monitoring the long-term impact of training. By implementing these practices, organizations can ensure that their investments in employee development yield substantial returns and contribute to overall business growth.

Examples of Comparative Analysis
Tech Industry Comparison: Infosys vs. TCS

- **Methodologies:** Both Infosys and TCS use the present value of future earnings method to quantify human resources. However, Infosys places a stronger emphasis on training and development costs, while TCS focuses on replacement costs during mergers and acquisitions.
- **Integration with Financial Reporting:** Infosys integrates HRA data into its financial statements to provide stakeholders with a comprehensive view of its assets. TCS uses HRA data to benchmark its performance against industry standards and communicate its human capital value to stakeholders.
- **Employee Engagement:** Infosys invests in extensive training programs through its Global Education Center, leading to higher employee satisfaction and retention. TCS focuses on diverse perspectives and data-driven audits to foster a positive work environment.

Healthcare Industry Comparison: Mayo Clinic vs. Cleveland Clinic

- **Methodologies:** Mayo Clinic uses cost-based methods, such as training and development costs, to measure the value of its human resources. Cleveland Clinic adopts value-based methods, such as economic value added (EVA), to quantify the contributions of its workforce.
- **Strategic HRM:** Both organizations align their HRA practices with strategic HRM goals. Mayo Clinic uses HRA data to support workforce planning and resource allocation, while Cleveland Clinic focuses on talent management and performance management systems.

- **Compliance and Risk Management:** Mayo Clinic ensures legal compliance through regular HR audits and data privacy measures. Cleveland Clinic uses HRA data to identify and mitigate HR-related risks, such as workforce shortages and skill gaps.

Financial Services Industry Comparison: JPMorgan Chase vs. Goldman Sachs

- **Methodologies:** JPMorgan Chase uses a combination of cost-based and value-based methods to measure the value of its human resources. Goldman Sachs focuses on value-based methods, such as the present value of future earnings and human asset multiplier.
- **Transparency and Disclosure:** Both organizations prioritize transparency in reporting HRA data. JPMorgan Chase integrates HRA data into its financial statements and provides comprehensive disclosures to stakeholders. Goldman Sachs focuses on clear communication of human resource values to enhance stakeholder perceptions.
- **Employee Retention:** JPMorgan Chase uses HRA data to develop effective retention strategies, such as competitive compensation packages and career development opportunities. Goldman Sachs focuses on employee well-being and engagement programs to reduce turnover and retain top talent.

Best Practices for Comparative Analysis

- **Standardize Measurement Methods:** Develop standardized methods and metrics for HRA to ensure consistency and comparability across different organizations and industries.
- **Benchmark Against Industry Standards:** Use industry standards and best practices as benchmarks for evaluating and improving HRA practices. Regularly review and update benchmarks to reflect changing market conditions.
- **Leverage Technology and Data Analytics:** Use technology and data analytics tools to enhance the accuracy and efficiency of HRA practices. Analyze data from multiple sources to gain comprehensive insights.
- **Promote Transparency and Disclosure:** Ensure transparency and clear communication in reporting HRA data. Provide stakeholders with

comprehensive disclosures to build trust and credibility.

- **Engage Stakeholders:** Involve key stakeholders, including HR professionals, managers, employees, and external auditors, in the HRA process. Seek their input and feedback to enhance the effectiveness of HRA practices.

Conclusion

Comparative analysis in Human Resource Accounting provides valuable insights into the effectiveness and impact of HRA practices across different organizations and industries. By evaluating methodologies, integration with financial reporting, strategic HRM, compliance, employee engagement, and cost management, organizations can identify best practices and benchmark their performance. The experiences of organizations like Infosys, TCS, Mayo Clinic, Cleveland Clinic, JPMorgan Chase, and Goldman Sachs offer valuable lessons for successfully implementing HRA and achieving sustainable growth.

CHAPTER TWENTY-EIGHT

FUTURE TRENDS AND DEVELOPMENTS

Introduction to Future Trends and Developments

Human Resource Accounting (HRA) is an evolving field that continues to develop as organizations recognize the importance of valuing human capital. Emerging trends and technological advancements are shaping the future of HRA, offering new opportunities for organizations to enhance their HR practices and optimize workforce management. This chapter explores the key future trends and developments in HRA and their potential impact on organizations.

Key Future Trends in Human Resource Accounting

Integration of Advanced Technologies

- **Artificial Intelligence (AI) and Machine Learning (ML):** Artificial Intelligence (AI) and Machine Learning (ML) are revolutionizing Human Resource Accounting (HRA) by automating data collection, analysis, and reporting. These technologies enable the processing of vast amounts of HR data to identify patterns, predict future outcomes, and provide actionable insights for decision-making.

  For instance, AI-powered analytics can analyze historical employee data to predict turnover rates, allowing organizations to implement proactive retention strategies. By understanding the factors contributing to turnover, such as job satisfaction, engagement levels, and career development opportunities, AI can recommend personalized interventions to enhance employee retention. Additionally, AI and ML can identify skill gaps, forecast workforce needs, and optimize talent management practices, ensuring the organization remains competitive and agile.

These technologies not only improve the efficiency and accuracy of HR processes but also empower HR professionals with data-driven insights to make informed decisions, ultimately driving organizational success.

- **Big Data Analytics:** Big data analytics revolutionizes Human Resource Accounting (HRA) by enabling organizations to analyze vast amounts of HR data from multiple sources, such as employee performance metrics, engagement surveys, and social media interactions. This comprehensive analysis offers a holistic view of workforce trends, skills gaps, and employee performance, providing valuable insights that can inform strategic HR decisions.

  By leveraging big data analytics, organizations can identify patterns and correlations that may not be evident through traditional analysis methods. For example, analyzing data on employee performance and engagement can reveal underlying factors that contribute to high turnover rates or low productivity. This information allows HR professionals to design targeted interventions and policies to address these issues, ultimately enhancing workforce stability and performance.

  Big data analytics also enhances the accuracy of human resource valuation methods by providing more precise and reliable data on employee contributions and potential. By incorporating a wide range of data points, such as training and development progress, project outcomes, and peer feedback, organizations can develop a more accurate and nuanced understanding of each employee's value to the organization. This improved accuracy supports better decision-making in areas such as compensation, promotions, and succession planning.

  Overall, the use of big data analytics in HRA empowers organizations to make informed, data-driven decisions that enhance workforce management, optimize talent utilization, and drive organizational success.

- **Blockchain Technology:** Blockchain technology revolutionizes HR data management by providing a secure and transparent framework for handling sensitive information. By leveraging blockchain, organizations can ensure the integrity and authenticity of HR records, including employee credentials, work history, and training certifications.

  The decentralized nature of blockchain means that data is stored across multiple nodes, making it tamper-proof and resistant to unauthorized changes. Each transaction or update is permanently recorded in the blockchain, ensuring that all data remains accurate and unaltered. This level of security enhances trust among employees and stakeholders, as they can be confident in the accuracy and reliability of the information.

Blockchain technology also streamlines the verification process for employee credentials and certifications. Employers can easily and securely verify the qualifications of potential hires without relying on third-party verification services, reducing time and administrative costs. Additionally, tracking training and development activities on the blockchain provides a transparent and immutable record of an employee's professional growth, supporting personalized development plans and career advancement.

Overall, blockchain technology enhances trust and accountability in HR practices by ensuring data integrity, improving verification processes, and providing a secure and transparent system for managing employee records.

Focus on Employee Well-being and Mental Health

- **Well-being Programs:** Organizations are increasingly recognizing the importance of employee well-being and mental health. HRA practices are evolving to include metrics that assess the impact of well-being programs on employee performance and productivity. For example, organizations may use HRA to evaluate the ROI of wellness initiatives and mental health support programs.
- **Flexible Work Arrangements:** The shift towards flexible work arrangements, such as remote work and flexible hours, is influencing HRA practices. Organizations are measuring the impact of flexible work on employee satisfaction, engagement, and productivity. HRA data supports the development of policies that promote work-life balance.

Sustainability and Corporate Social Responsibility (CSR)

- **Sustainable HR Practices:** Organizations are integrating sustainability and CSR into their HR practices. HRA is being used to measure the impact of sustainable HR initiatives, such as eco-friendly workplace policies and community engagement programs. For example, HRA can assess the value of reducing the organization's carbon footprint through remote work options.

- **Diversity, Equity, and Inclusion (DEI):** HRA practices are incorporating metrics to evaluate the effectiveness of DEI initiatives. Organizations are using HRA data to track diversity in hiring, pay equity, and employee inclusion. HRA supports the development of strategies to promote a diverse and inclusive workplace.

Global Workforce Management

- **Cross-Border HR Practices:** The increasing globalization of the workforce is driving the need for cross-border HR practices. HRA is evolving to address the challenges and opportunities presented by a diverse and geographically dispersed workforce. For example, organizations are using HRA to evaluate the cost and benefits of international assignments and remote work.
- **Cultural Competence:** HRA practices are incorporating metrics to assess cultural competence and cross-cultural collaboration. Organizations are measuring the impact of cultural training programs and initiatives that promote understanding and respect among employees from different cultural backgrounds.

Real-Time Data and Predictive Analytics

- **Real-Time HR Insights:** The use of real-time data in HRA provides organizations with immediate insights into workforce trends and performance. Real-time analytics enable organizations to make proactive HR decisions and respond quickly to emerging issues. For example, real-time data can be used to monitor employee engagement and address concerns promptly.
- **Predictive Analytics:** Predictive analytics in HRA leverages historical data to forecast future workforce trends and outcomes. Organizations are using predictive models to anticipate employee turnover, identify high-potential employees, and plan for future talent needs. Predictive analytics enhances strategic HR planning and decision-making.

Impact of Future Trends on Organizations

- **Enhanced Decision-Making:** The integration of advanced technologies and data analytics in HRA enhances decision-making by providing accurate, real-time, and predictive insights. Organizations can make informed HR decisions that align with strategic goals and optimize workforce management.
- **Improved Employee Experience:** The focus on employee well-being, mental health, and flexible work arrangements enhances the overall employee experience. HRA practices that measure and support these initiatives contribute to higher levels of employee satisfaction, engagement, and retention.
- **Sustainable and Inclusive Practices:** The incorporation of sustainability and DEI metrics in HRA promotes sustainable and inclusive HR practices. Organizations can develop and implement strategies that foster a positive and equitable work environment, enhancing their reputation and social responsibility.
- **Global Competitiveness:** The ability to manage a global workforce effectively through cross-border HR practices and cultural competence enhances organizations' global competitiveness. HRA supports the development of strategies that leverage the strengths of a diverse and dispersed workforce.
- **Proactive HR Management:** The use of real-time data and predictive analytics enables organizations to adopt a proactive approach to HR management. Organizations can anticipate and address HR challenges before they escalate, ensuring a resilient and agile workforce.

Conclusion

The future of Human Resource Accounting is being shaped by emerging trends and technological advancements that offer new opportunities for organizations to enhance their HR practices. By integrating advanced technologies, focusing on employee well-being, promoting sustainability and inclusion, managing a global workforce, and leveraging real-time data and predictive analytics, organizations can optimize their workforce management and achieve sustainable growth. The evolving landscape of HRA presents exciting possibilities for organizations committed to valuing and maximizing their human capital.

CHAPTER TWENTY-NINE

Technological Advancements

Introduction to Technological Advancements

The rapid advancement of technology has significantly transformed Human Resource Accounting (HRA) by enhancing data collection, analysis, reporting, and overall decision-making processes. These technological innovations enable organizations to gain deeper insights into their human capital, optimize HR practices, and drive strategic growth. This chapter explores the key technological advancements shaping the future of HRA and their impact on organizational performance.

Key Technological Advancements in HRA

Artificial Intelligence (AI) and Machine Learning (ML)

- **AI-Powered Analytics:** AI-powered analytics are transforming Human Resource Accounting (HRA) by streamlining data collection and analysis processes. Leveraging artificial intelligence (AI) and machine learning (ML) technologies, organizations can efficiently process vast amounts of HR data, identifying patterns and generating actionable insights. These technologies enable a deeper understanding of workforce dynamics, allowing HR professionals to make informed decisions.

  For instance, AI can analyze employee performance data to predict future trends, such as turnover rates and potential skill gaps. By identifying employees who are at risk of leaving and pinpointing areas where additional training is needed, organizations can proactively address these challenges. This predictive capability enhances workforce planning and ensures that the organization is prepared to meet future demands.

Furthermore, AI-powered analytics can uncover hidden correlations and trends that may not be apparent through traditional analysis methods. This advanced insight allows organizations to optimize their HR strategies, improve employee engagement, and ultimately drive better organizational performance. Overall, the integration of AI and ML technologies into HRA offers a powerful toolset for enhancing HR management and maximizing the value of human capital.

- **Personalized Employee Development:** Personalized Employee Development leverages AI-driven platforms to create customized training and development plans tailored to individual employees' performance and learning preferences. By analyzing data on employee strengths, weaknesses, and career aspirations, these platforms can recommend specific development programs that align with each employee's unique needs.

This personalized approach ensures that employees receive targeted training that directly addresses their skill gaps and enhances their existing abilities. Additionally, by catering to individual learning styles, AI-driven platforms can optimize the effectiveness of training programs, making the learning experience more engaging and impactful.

Organizations benefit from this tailored development by seeing improvements in employee skills and productivity. Employees who receive relevant and personalized training are more likely to feel valued and motivated, leading to increased job satisfaction and retention. Ultimately, personalized employee development drives better performance, fosters continuous growth, and contributes to the organization's overall success.

Big Data Analytics

- **Comprehensive Data Analysis:** Comprehensive data analysis through big data analytics empowers organizations to examine extensive volumes of HR data from a variety of sources. By integrating data from employee performance metrics, engagement surveys, social media interactions, and other relevant inputs, organizations can achieve a holistic view of workforce trends and behaviors. This multifaceted analysis helps uncover patterns and correlations that might otherwise go unnoticed, enabling more informed decision-making.

For example, analyzing engagement surveys alongside performance data can reveal insights into what drives employee satisfaction and productivity. Social media interactions can provide additional context about employee sentiment and organizational culture. By leveraging these diverse data sources, organizations can identify trends related to retention, performance, and overall employee well-being. This comprehensive approach not only enhances HR strategies but also supports the development of targeted interventions to improve workforce engagement, efficiency, and satisfaction.

Ultimately, the ability to analyze and interpret large volumes of HR data through big data analytics allows organizations to proactively address challenges, capitalize on opportunities, and maintain a competitive edge in the ever-evolving business landscape.

- **Predictive Analytics:** Predictive analytics is a powerful tool that leverages big data analytics to forecast future HR trends, enabling organizations to make proactive decisions and strategic plans. By analyzing historical and current HR data, predictive models can identify patterns and correlations that help forecast key metrics such as employee turnover, absenteeism, and performance outcomes.

For instance, predictive analytics can identify factors that contribute to high turnover rates, allowing organizations to address underlying issues and implement retention strategies before problems escalate. Similarly, by forecasting absenteeism trends, organizations can plan for potential staffing shortages and ensure adequate coverage. Predictive analytics also helps in evaluating performance outcomes, enabling managers to identify high-potential employees and tailor development programs to nurture their growth.

Overall, predictive analytics provides organizations with valuable insights that support data-driven HR planning and decision-making. By anticipating future trends, businesses can proactively manage their workforce, optimize resources, and enhance overall organizational performance. This forward-looking approach ensures that organizations remain agile and responsive to changing market demands and internal dynamics.

Blockchain Technology

- **Secure Data Management:** Blockchain technology provides a secure and transparent solution for managing HR records, ensuring the integrity and authenticity of employee data. By using a decentralized and immutable ledger, blockchain offers a robust way to store and verify information such as credentials, work history, and training certifications. This technology enhances trust by allowing only authorized parties to access and update records, while every change is permanently recorded and cannot be altered. As a result, the risk of data tampering is significantly reduced, providing greater confidence in the accuracy and reliability of HR records. Additionally, blockchain's transparency ensures that all stakeholders have a clear view of the data, promoting accountability and compliance with regulatory requirements. Overall, blockchain technology offers a powerful tool for secure data management, safeguarding employee information and enhancing the efficiency of HR processes.

- **Decentralized HR Systems:** Decentralized HR systems powered by blockchain technology revolutionize the management of employee data by giving control back to the employees. In a decentralized system, employees have ownership and control over their personal information, such as credentials, work history, and training certifications. This approach empowers employees to manage their own data, ensuring that it is accurate and up-to-date.

  The use of blockchain technology enhances data privacy and security by creating an immutable and transparent ledger where only authorized parties can access and update information. Each transaction or update is permanently recorded on the blockchain, making it tamper-proof and ensuring data integrity. This reduces the risk of unauthorized access, data breaches, and fraud, providing a secure environment for sensitive HR data.

  Additionally, decentralized HR systems can streamline processes such as recruitment, onboarding, and verification of credentials. Employers can easily verify the authenticity of an employee's qualifications and work history without relying on third-party verification services, saving time and reducing administrative costs.

  Overall, decentralized HR systems powered by blockchain technology offer a more secure, transparent, and efficient way to manage employee data, fostering trust and empowering employees in the process.

Cloud Computing

- **Scalable HR Solutions:** Scalable HR solutions enabled by cloud computing offer numerous advantages for modern organizations. By utilizing cloud-based HR platforms, organizations can store and access HR data from anywhere at any time, providing unparalleled flexibility and convenience. This capability is particularly beneficial for remote and distributed teams, ensuring seamless access to essential HR information regardless of location.

  Cloud-based HR solutions are also highly scalable, allowing organizations to adjust their usage and resources as needed. This flexibility means that HR systems can easily accommodate growth or changes in the workforce without the need for significant infrastructure investments. Additionally, cloud computing reduces the burden of maintaining on-premises hardware and software, resulting in cost savings and enhanced operational efficiency.

  Furthermore, cloud-based HR platforms often come with integrated tools and features that streamline various HR processes, such as recruitment, onboarding, performance management, and employee development. These platforms provide a centralized and cohesive environment for managing the entire employee lifecycle, improving data accuracy and decision-making.

  Overall, scalable HR solutions powered by cloud computing offer a cost-effective, flexible, and efficient way to manage workforce data and HR processes, supporting organizational agility and growth.
- **Collaborative Tools:** Collaborative tools powered by cloud computing are revolutionizing the way HR teams, managers, and employees work together. These tools facilitate seamless communication and data sharing, enabling real-time collaboration across different locations and time zones. For instance, cloud-based platforms often include shared dashboards that provide a centralized view of key HR metrics and performance indicators. This transparency allows everyone involved to stay informed and aligned with organizational goals.

  Real-time analytics further enhance collaboration by providing up-to-date insights into various HR functions, such as employee engagement, performance, and recruitment. These analytics enable HR teams and managers to make informed decisions quickly, based on the latest data. Additionally, cloud-based tools support document sharing, video conferencing, and instant messaging, making it easy for teams to collaborate on projects, conduct meetings, and communicate efficiently.

Overall, cloud computing's collaborative tools create a connected and cohesive work environment, fostering teamwork, enhancing productivity, and driving better outcomes for the organization.

Internet of Things (IoT)

- **Workplace Monitoring:** Workplace monitoring through IoT (Internet of Things) devices is transforming how organizations optimize their work environments. These devices can track various conditions such as temperature, lighting, air quality, and employee movement, providing valuable data to create a more comfortable and productive workspace.

  For instance, smart thermostats can adjust temperature settings based on occupancy and preferences, ensuring a consistent and comfortable climate. Intelligent lighting systems can modify brightness and color temperature to match the time of day and the needs of the employees, reducing eye strain and boosting productivity.

  Furthermore, IoT devices can monitor employee movement and space utilization, helping organizations design layouts that promote better workflow and collaboration. By understanding how spaces are used, companies can make informed decisions about workspace design, ensuring that areas are efficiently utilized and conducive to teamwork.

  Additionally, workplace monitoring can enhance safety by detecting hazards such as poor air quality or potential equipment malfunctions, allowing for timely interventions to prevent accidents and maintain a healthy environment.

  Overall, IoT-driven workplace monitoring provides organizations with actionable insights to create an optimal work environment, fostering employee well-being and enhancing overall productivity.

- **Health and Safety:** IoT-enabled wearables are transforming workplace health and safety by providing real-time tracking of employee health metrics, such as heart rate, activity levels, and even stress indicators. By collecting and analyzing this data, organizations can gain valuable insights into the well-being of their workforce and take proactive measures to promote employee health.

  For example, wearables can alert employees and managers to potential health issues, such as elevated heart rates or signs of fatigue, allowing for timely interventions. This can help prevent workplace injuries and promote a safer work environment. Additionally, organizations can use the data to design personalized wellness programs, encouraging employees to engage in healthy behaviors and activities that improve their overall well-being.

Moreover, IoT-enabled wearables can monitor environmental conditions, such as air quality and temperature, ensuring that the workplace remains conducive to health and productivity. By leveraging this technology, organizations can implement targeted health and safety initiatives that not only comply with regulatory requirements but also enhance employee satisfaction and retention. Overall, IoT-enabled wearables offer a powerful tool for creating a safer, healthier, and more supportive work environment.

Robotic Process Automation (RPA)

- **Automating HR Tasks:** Robotic Process Automation (RPA) technology is revolutionizing human resources by automating repetitive and time-consuming tasks. By using software robots to handle routine HR functions such as payroll processing, benefits administration, and data entry, organizations can significantly improve operational efficiency. RPA ensures accuracy, reduces errors, and saves valuable time, allowing HR professionals to shift their focus from administrative work to more strategic activities. This enables HR teams to engage in higher-value tasks, such as talent management, employee development, and organizational planning, ultimately contributing to the overall success and growth of the organization.
- **Enhanced Accuracy:** Enhanced accuracy in HR processes is one of the significant benefits of Robotic Process Automation (RPA). By automating routine tasks such as data entry, payroll processing, and benefits administration, RPA minimizes the risk of human errors that can occur due to manual handling. This ensures that HR processes are executed with a high degree of precision and consistency.

Moreover, RPA helps organizations maintain compliance with regulations by accurately capturing and processing data according to established standards. Automated systems can be programmed to adhere to legal and regulatory requirements, reducing the likelihood of non-compliance and potential penalties. This enhanced accuracy not only improves the reliability of HR operations but also builds trust among employees and stakeholders, knowing that their data is managed meticulously.

Ultimately, RPA's ability to enhance accuracy and compliance allows HR professionals to focus on strategic initiatives and value-added activities, contributing to the overall efficiency and effectiveness of the HR function.

Impact of Technological Advancements on HRA

Enhanced Decision-Making

Data-Driven Insights: Technological advancements provide HR professionals with data-driven insights that support informed decision-making. By leveraging AI, big data analytics, and predictive models, organizations can make strategic HR decisions that align with organizational goals.

Improved Efficiency and Productivity

Automation of HR Processes: Technologies like RPA and AI automate routine HR tasks, improving efficiency and freeing up HR professionals to focus on value-added activities. This enhances overall productivity and reduces operational costs.

Scalable Solutions: Cloud computing and scalable HR solutions enable organizations to efficiently manage their workforce, regardless of size or location. This flexibility supports growth and adaptability.

Enhanced Employee Experience

Personalized Development: AI-driven platforms personalize employee training and development plans, enhancing the employee experience and promoting continuous learning and growth.

Well-Being and Safety: IoT devices and health monitoring tools promote employee well-being and safety, contributing to a positive work environment and higher job satisfaction.

Greater Transparency and Security

Secure Data Management: Blockchain technology ensures the security and authenticity of HR data, enhancing trust and reducing the risk of data breaches.

Transparent Reporting: Technological advancements enable transparent and accurate reporting of HR data, providing stakeholders with a clear view of workforce trends and performance.

Proactive HR Management

Predictive Analytics: Predictive analytics supports proactive HR management by forecasting future trends and identifying potential issues before they escalate. This enables organizations to take preventive measures and ensure a resilient workforce.

Case Studies and Practical Examples

Google: Google leverages AI and big data analytics to gain insights into employee performance, engagement, and development. The company's AI-powered platforms personalize training programs and recommend tailored development plans for employees.

IBM: IBM uses blockchain technology to verify employee credentials and track training and development activities. This ensures data integrity and transparency in HR records.

General Electric (GE): GE utilizes IoT devices to monitor workplace conditions and track employee health metrics. This data supports initiatives to enhance employee well-being and optimize the work environment.

Conclusion

Technological advancements are transforming Human Resource Accounting by enhancing data collection, analysis, reporting, and decision-making processes. The integration of AI, big data analytics, blockchain, cloud computing, IoT, and RPA offers organizations new opportunities to optimize their HR practices and drive strategic growth. By leveraging these technologies, organizations can gain deeper insights into their human capital, improve efficiency and productivity, enhance the employee experience, and ensure greater transparency and security. The future of HRA is poised to be shaped by these innovations, offering exciting possibilities for organizations committed to valuing and maximizing their human capital.

CHAPTER THIRTY

GLOBAL PERSPECTIVES

Introduction to Global Perspectives

Human Resource Accounting (HRA) is practiced around the world, with varying approaches, methodologies, and regulations influenced by regional, cultural, and economic factors. Understanding global perspectives on HRA provides valuable insights into how different countries and organizations value and manage their human capital. This chapter explores the key global perspectives on HRA, highlighting the similarities and differences across various regions and industries.

Key Global Perspectives on HRA

North America

United States: In the United States, HRA practices are driven by the need for transparency, accountability, and compliance with financial reporting standards. Organizations often use cost-based methods, such as historical cost and replacement cost, as well as value-based methods like the present value of future earnings. The emphasis is on integrating HRA data into financial statements to provide stakeholders with a comprehensive view of organizational assets.

Canada: Canadian organizations focus on aligning HRA with strategic HRM goals and enhancing employee well-being. There is a strong emphasis on employee engagement, diversity, and inclusion. HRA practices often include metrics for assessing the impact of well-being programs and DEI initiatives on employee performance and satisfaction.

Europe

United Kingdom: In the UK, HRA is influenced by both financial reporting standards and corporate governance requirements. Organizations prioritize transparency and disclosure of human capital data. HRA practices often involve value-based methods, such as economic value added (EVA) and human asset multiplier, to quantify the contributions of employees.

Germany: German organizations emphasize the integration of HRA with overall organizational performance. There is a focus on continuous improvement, employee development, and compliance with labor laws. HRA practices often include detailed evaluations of training and development programs and their ROI.

France: In France, HRA practices are influenced by regulations related to employee rights, labor relations, and social responsibility. Organizations use HRA to assess the impact of HR practices on employee well-being, engagement, and organizational culture. There is a strong emphasis on work-life balance and employee satisfaction.

Asia-Pacific

India: Indian organizations are increasingly adopting HRA practices to enhance strategic HRM and workforce management. There is a focus on training and development, talent management, and employee engagement. Organizations like Infosys and TCS use a combination of cost-based and value-based methods to quantify human resources and support strategic decision-making.

China: In China, HRA practices are influenced by the rapid economic growth and evolving labor market. Organizations prioritize talent management, workforce planning, and compliance with labor regulations. HRA practices often include metrics for assessing employee performance, productivity, and development.

Japan: Japanese organizations emphasize lifelong employment, employee loyalty, and continuous improvement. HRA practices focus on measuring the value of employee development, training programs, and organizational culture. There is a strong emphasis on teamwork, collaboration, and employee well-being.

Middle East

United Arab Emirates (UAE): In the UAE, HRA practices are influenced by the diverse and multicultural workforce. Organizations focus on talent management, employee engagement, and compliance with labor laws. HRA practices often include metrics for assessing the impact of training and development programs on employee performance and retention.

Saudi Arabia: Saudi organizations are increasingly adopting HRA practices to support economic diversification and workforce localization initiatives. There is a focus on employee development, compliance with labor regulations, and alignment with national strategic goals. HRA practices often include evaluations of employee training programs and their impact on organizational performance.

Africa

South Africa: In South Africa, HRA practices are influenced by regulations related to employment equity, skills development, and social responsibility. Organizations use HRA to assess the impact of HR practices on diversity, inclusion, and employee development. There is a strong emphasis on aligning HR practices with national economic and social goals.

Nigeria: Nigerian organizations are increasingly recognizing the importance of HRA for strategic HRM and workforce planning. There is a focus on employee development, talent management, and compliance with labor laws. HRA practices often include metrics for assessing employee performance, engagement, and retention.

Common Themes Across Global Perspectives

Emphasis on Employee Well-being and Development: Across regions, there is a growing recognition of the importance of employee well-being and development. HRA practices often include metrics for assessing the impact of well-being programs, training initiatives, and career development on employee performance and satisfaction.

Integration with Financial Reporting: Organizations worldwide are integrating HRA data into financial statements to provide stakeholders with a comprehensive view of organizational assets. This enhances transparency, accountability, and informed decision-making.

Focus on Compliance and Risk Management: Compliance with labor laws, employment regulations, and industry standards is a common theme across regions. HRA practices help organizations identify and mitigate HR-related risks, ensuring legal compliance and reducing the risk of penalties.

Promotion of Diversity, Equity, and Inclusion (DEI): DEI is a key focus for organizations globally. HRA practices often include metrics for assessing diversity in hiring, pay equity, and employee inclusion. This supports the development of strategies to promote a diverse and inclusive workplace.

Adoption of Advanced Technologies: Organizations are leveraging advanced technologies, such as AI, big data analytics, and blockchain, to enhance HRA practices. These technologies provide accurate, real-time, and predictive insights that support strategic HRM and workforce management.

Conclusion

Global perspectives on Human Resource Accounting reveal both similarities and differences in how organizations value and manage their human capital. Understanding these perspectives provides valuable insights into the diverse approaches, methodologies, and regulations influencing HRA practices worldwide. By adopting best practices and leveraging advanced technologies, organizations can enhance their HRA practices, optimize workforce management, and achieve sustainable growth. The evolving landscape of HRA presents exciting possibilities for organizations committed to valuing and maximizing their human capital in a globalized world.

CHAPTER THIRTY-ONE

EMERGING PRACTICES

Introduction to Emerging Practices

Human Resource Accounting (HRA) is continually evolving, with new practices and methodologies emerging to address the changing needs of organizations and the dynamic nature of the workforce. These emerging practices are driven by advancements in technology, shifts in organizational priorities, and the growing recognition of the value of human capital. This chapter explores the key emerging practices in HRA and their potential impact on organizations.

Key Emerging Practices in HRA

Holistic Human Capital Management

Integrated Approach: Organizations are adopting a holistic approach to human capital management that integrates HRA with other HR functions, such as talent management, performance management, and employee engagement. This approach provides a comprehensive view of the workforce and supports strategic decision-making.

Human Capital Ecosystem: The concept of a human capital ecosystem emphasizes the interconnectedness of various HR practices and their collective impact on organizational performance. Organizations are using HRA to assess and optimize the entire ecosystem, from recruitment and onboarding to development and retention.

Employee Experience and Engagement Metrics

Employee Experience: Organizations are increasingly focusing on measuring and enhancing the employee experience. HRA practices now include metrics that assess various aspects of the employee experience, such as job satisfaction, work-life balance, and organizational culture.

Engagement Analytics: Advanced analytics tools are being used to measure employee engagement in real-time. By analyzing data from surveys, social media, and other sources, organizations can gain insights into engagement levels and identify areas for improvement.

Diversity, Equity, and Inclusion (DEI) Metrics

Comprehensive DEI Metrics: Organizations are developing comprehensive DEI metrics to assess the effectiveness of their diversity and inclusion initiatives. These metrics go beyond basic demographic data to include measures of inclusion, belonging, and equity in opportunities and compensation.

Impact Assessment: HRA practices are evolving to assess the impact of DEI initiatives on organizational performance. This includes evaluating the correlation between DEI efforts and key performance indicators (KPIs), such as innovation, productivity, and employee retention.

Sustainable HR Practices

Environmental, Social, and Governance (ESG) Reporting: Organizations are integrating HRA with ESG reporting to demonstrate their commitment to sustainability and social responsibility. HRA practices now include metrics that assess the impact of sustainable HR initiatives, such as remote work policies, green workplace practices, and community engagement programs.

Sustainable Workforce Development: HRA is being used to support sustainable workforce development by measuring the long-term impact of training and development programs on employee growth and organizational performance.

AI-Driven HR Analytics

Predictive HR Analytics: AI-driven HR analytics tools are being used to predict future workforce trends, such as turnover, absenteeism, and performance outcomes. Predictive models help organizations make proactive HR decisions and implement preventive measures.

Sentiment Analysis: AI-powered sentiment analysis tools analyze employee feedback from surveys, emails, and social media to gauge sentiment and identify emerging issues. This real-time analysis supports timely interventions to enhance employee well-being and engagement.

Blockchain for Credential Verification

Credential Verification: Blockchain technology is being used to securely verify employee credentials, such as educational qualifications, certifications, and work experience. This enhances data integrity and reduces the risk of fraud.

Decentralized HR Records: Blockchain enables the creation of decentralized HR records where employees have control over their own data. This empowers employees and enhances data privacy and security.

Wellness and Mental Health Metrics

Holistic Wellness Programs: Organizations are expanding their wellness programs to include mental health support, stress management, and holistic well-being. HRA practices now include metrics that assess the impact of these programs on employee health and productivity.

Real-Time Health Data: IoT-enabled wearables and health monitoring tools provide real-time health data that can be used to support wellness initiatives. Organizations are using this data to promote a healthy and safe work environment.

Impact of Emerging Practices on Organizations

Enhanced Employee Experience: By focusing on employee experience and engagement metrics, organizations can create a positive work environment that enhances job satisfaction, retention, and overall performance.

Increased Transparency and Accountability: The integration of DEI metrics and ESG reporting into HRA practices enhances transparency and accountability. Organizations can demonstrate their commitment to diversity, inclusion, and sustainability, building trust with stakeholders.

Proactive HR Management: AI-driven HR analytics and predictive models enable organizations to adopt a proactive approach to HR management. By anticipating future trends and addressing emerging issues, organizations can ensure a resilient and agile workforce.

Data Integrity and Security: The use of blockchain for credential verification and decentralized HR records enhances data integrity and security. Organizations can build trust with employees by ensuring the accuracy and privacy of their data.

Support for Well-Being: By incorporating wellness and mental health metrics into HRA practices, organizations can support holistic employee well-being. This leads to higher levels of engagement, productivity, and overall organizational performance.

Case Studies and Practical Examples

SAP: SAP uses AI-driven HR analytics to predict employee turnover and identify key drivers of engagement. The company's focus on real-time analytics supports proactive HR management and enhances employee retention.

Unilever: Unilever integrates DEI metrics and ESG reporting into its HRA practices. The company's commitment to sustainability and social responsibility is demonstrated through comprehensive reporting and transparent communication with stakeholders.

PwC: PwC uses blockchain technology for credential verification, ensuring the integrity and authenticity of employee data. This reduces the risk of fraud and enhances data security.

Conclusion

Emerging practices in Human Resource Accounting are transforming how organizations value and manage their human capital. By adopting a holistic approach, integrating advanced technologies, and focusing on key areas such as employee experience, DEI, sustainability, and well-being, organizations can optimize their HR practices and drive strategic growth. The evolving landscape of HRA presents exciting opportunities for organizations committed to enhancing their workforce management and achieving sustainable success.

CHAPTER THIRTY-TWO

CONCLUSION

Summary of Human Resource Accounting (HRA)

Human Resource Accounting (HRA) is a critical field that focuses on measuring and reporting the value of an organization's human resources. By recognizing the economic contributions of employees, HRA provides valuable insights that support strategic decision-making, enhance transparency, and optimize workforce management.

Throughout this book, we have explored various aspects of HRA, including its concepts, methodologies, applications, and challenges. We have delved into the integration of HRA with financial reporting, strategic HRM, performance evaluation, and compliance. Additionally, we have examined emerging practices, technological advancements, and global perspectives in HRA.

Key Takeaways

Importance of Human Capital: Human capital is a vital asset for organizations, contributing significantly to overall performance and success. HRA helps quantify this value, providing a more comprehensive view of organizational assets.

Methodologies and Approaches: HRA employs various methodologies, including cost-based methods (e.g., historical cost, replacement cost) and value-based methods (e.g., present value of future earnings, economic value added). These methods offer different perspectives on the financial worth of human resources.

Integration with Financial Reporting: Integrating HRA data into financial statements enhances transparency and accountability. This integration provides stakeholders with a clear understanding of the value and contributions of human resources.

Strategic HRM and Decision-Making: HRA supports strategic HRM by providing data-driven insights into workforce trends, skills gaps, and potential areas for investment. This information helps organizations align their HR practices with strategic goals and make informed decisions.

Technological Advancements: Technological innovations, such as AI, big data analytics, blockchain, cloud computing, and IoT, are transforming HRA. These technologies enhance data collection, analysis, and reporting, providing accurate and actionable insights.

Emerging Practices: Emerging practices in HRA, such as holistic human capital management, employee experience metrics, DEI metrics, and sustainable HR practices, are shaping the future of the field. These practices address the evolving needs of organizations and the dynamic nature of the workforce.

Global Perspectives: Understanding global perspectives on HRA reveals diverse approaches, methodologies, and regulations influenced by regional, cultural, and economic factors. By adopting best practices and leveraging advanced technologies, organizations can enhance their HRA practices and achieve sustainable growth.

Future Outlook

The future of HRA is promising, with continued advancements in technology and evolving organizational priorities driving innovation. Organizations that effectively implement HRA practices will be better positioned to optimize their workforce management, enhance employee well-being, and achieve strategic goals.

As HRA continues to evolve, it will play an increasingly important role in helping organizations navigate the complexities of the modern workforce. By valuing and maximizing their human capital, organizations can drive innovation, competitiveness, and sustainable success.

CHAPTER THIRTY-THREE

SUMMARY OF KEY POINTS

Overview of Human Resource Accounting (HRA)

Human Resource Accounting (HRA) is a specialized field that focuses on identifying, measuring, and reporting the value of an organization's human resources. By quantifying the economic contributions of employees, HRA provides valuable insights that support strategic decision-making, enhance transparency, and optimize workforce management.

Key Points Covered in the Book

Concept and Scope of HRA

- HRA aims to provide a more accurate representation of an organization's assets by including the value of human resources.
- It involves quantifying the financial worth of employees' skills, knowledge, and abilities using various measurement methods.

Measurement and Valuation Methods

- **Cost-Based Methods:** Historical cost, replacement cost, and training and development cost.
- **Value-Based Methods:** Present value of future earnings, economic value added (EVA), and human asset multiplier.

Each method offers different perspectives on the value of human resources.

Integration with Financial Reporting

- Integrating HRA data into financial statements enhances transparency and accountability.
- This integration provides stakeholders with a comprehensive view of organizational assets and performance.

Strategic Human Resource Management (HRM)

- HRA supports strategic HRM by providing data-driven insights into workforce trends, skills gaps, and potential areas for investment.
- This information helps organizations align their HR practices with strategic goals and make informed decisions.

Performance Evaluation and Compensation

- HRA offers a framework for evaluating employee performance and contributions.
- It supports the design of incentive compensation and reward systems that align employee interests with organizational goals.

Technological Advancements

- Technologies like AI, big data analytics, blockchain, cloud computing, and IoT are transforming HRA.
- These advancements enhance data collection, analysis, reporting, and decision-making processes.

Emerging Practices

- Holistic human capital management, employee experience metrics, DEI metrics, sustainable HR practices, AI-driven HR analytics, and wellness metrics are shaping the future of HRA.
- These practices address the evolving needs of organizations and the dynamic nature of the workforce.

Global Perspectives

- Understanding global perspectives on HRA reveals diverse approaches, methodologies, and regulations influenced by regional, cultural, and economic factors.

- Adopting best practices and leveraging advanced technologies can enhance HRA practices and achieve sustainable growth.

Challenges and Limitations

- Data availability and accuracy, subjectivity and bias, lack of standardization, and cost and complexity are common challenges in HRA.
- Addressing these challenges is essential for effective implementation and accurate reporting of human resources.

Implementation and Best Practices

- Successful implementation of HRA requires leadership support, pilot programs, comprehensive frameworks, technological integration, data privacy, stakeholder engagement, and continuous monitoring.
- Best practices include aligning HRA with organizational goals, standardizing methods, promoting transparency, and focusing on continuous improvement.

Conclusion

Human Resource Accounting is a valuable tool for recognizing and quantifying the economic value of an organization's human resources. By integrating HRA into financial reporting, strategic HRM, performance evaluation, and other HR functions, organizations can enhance their decision-making, transparency, and overall performance. The evolving landscape of HRA, shaped by technological advancements and emerging practices, offers exciting opportunities for organizations committed to valuing and maximizing their human capital.

CHAPTER THIRTY-FOUR

FUTURE RESEARCH DIRECTIONS

Introduction to Future Research Directions

As the field of Human Resource Accounting (HRA) continues to evolve, there are numerous opportunities for further research to advance our understanding and application of HRA practices. Future research in HRA can explore new methodologies, address existing challenges, and uncover innovative ways to measure and manage human capital. This chapter outlines key areas for future research in HRA and highlights their potential contributions to the field.

Key Areas for Future Research

Advanced Measurement Techniques

AI and Machine Learning in HRA: Research can explore the application of artificial intelligence (AI) and machine learning (ML) algorithms in developing advanced measurement techniques for HRA. This includes predictive models for employee performance, turnover, and engagement.

Enhanced Valuation Methods: Investigate new and improved valuation methods that account for both tangible and intangible aspects of human resources. This includes exploring hybrid models that combine cost-based and value-based approaches.

Impact of Technological Advancements

- **Blockchain Technology:** Examine the potential of blockchain technology in securely managing HR data, verifying credentials, and enhancing transparency in HRA practices.

- **IoT and Real-Time Data:** Investigate the use of Internet of Things (IoT) devices for real-time data collection on employee health, safety, and productivity. Assess the impact of real-time data on HR decision-making and employee well-being.

Employee Well-being and Mental Health

- **Well-being Metrics:** Develop comprehensive metrics to assess the impact of well-being programs, mental health support, and stress management initiatives on employee performance and organizational outcomes.
- **Work-Life Balance:** Research the effects of work-life balance initiatives, such as flexible work arrangements and remote work, on employee satisfaction, engagement, and productivity.

Diversity, Equity, and Inclusion (DEI)

- **DEI Metrics and Impact:** Investigate the development of advanced DEI metrics that go beyond demographic data to include measures of inclusion, belonging, and equity in opportunities. Assess the impact of DEI initiatives on organizational performance and innovation.
- **Inclusive Leadership:** Explore the role of inclusive leadership in promoting diversity and fostering an inclusive workplace culture. Evaluate the impact of leadership development programs on DEI outcomes.

Sustainable HR Practices

- **Environmental, Social, and Governance (ESG) Integration:** Research the integration of HRA with ESG reporting to demonstrate organizational commitment to sustainability and social responsibility. Assess the impact of sustainable HR practices on employee engagement and organizational reputation.
- **Long-Term Workforce Development:** Investigate strategies for sustainable workforce development that focus on long-term employee growth, skill enhancement, and career progression.

Global Perspectives and Cross-Cultural HRA

- **Cross-Cultural Comparisons:** Conduct comparative studies on HRA practices across different countries and cultures. Examine how regional, cultural, and economic factors influence HRA methodologies and outcomes.
- **Global Workforce Management:** Research best practices for managing a global workforce, including cross-border HR practices, cultural competence, and international talent management. Assess the impact of globalization on HRA.

Integration with Financial Reporting

- **Standardization of HRA Reporting:** Explore the development of standardized frameworks and guidelines for integrating HRA data into financial statements. Assess the impact of standardized reporting on transparency and stakeholder perceptions.
- **Impact on Financial Performance:** Investigate the correlation between the inclusion of HRA data in financial statements and overall financial performance. Evaluate how stakeholders use HRA information in their decision-making processes.

Ethical Considerations in HRA

- **Data Privacy and Confidentiality:** Research best practices for ensuring data privacy and confidentiality in HRA. Examine the ethical implications of data collection, analysis, and reporting in HRA practices.
- **Fairness and Equity:** Investigate the role of HRA in promoting fairness and equity in HR practices. Assess the impact of transparent and unbiased HRA methods on employee trust and organizational culture.

Conclusion

Future research in Human Resource Accounting offers exciting opportunities to advance the field and enhance our understanding of human capital management. By exploring advanced measurement techniques, the impact of technological advancements, employee well-being, DEI, sustainable HR practices, global perspectives, integration with financial reporting, and ethical considerations, researchers can contribute to the development of innovative and effective HRA practices. These research directions have the potential to shape the future of HRA and support organizations in valuing and maximizing their human capital.

www.ingramcontent.com/pod-product-compliance
Lightning Source LLC
Chambersburg PA
CBHW031021160726
47991CB00005B/1818